D0922281

wild sourdough

wild
sourdough
the natural way to bake

YOKE MARDEWI

NEW HOLLAND

To my precious daughter, Dechen,
and all future home-bakers

Contents

Introduction

We need the same things to bake bread that we need to build character:

We need the right proportion of ingredients—not too much of this or too little of that.

We need an animating principle, like the yeast or leaven—something to enliven us, a passion.

We need to be kneaded, mixed well by the slow, rhythmic pattern of everyday life.

Periodically, we need to rest in a warm place with a towel over our heads.

We need to be punched down, sometimes at the peak of our rising.

And we need to be tested in the fires of suffering.

Ultimately, our lives are without meaning until we're broken and shared.

We're not meant to sit on the shelf but to be given away.

Father Dominic Garramone, *On Bread and You*

My wish in writing this book is to inspire you to go into your kitchen with some beautiful flours and start experimenting. Breadmaking at home is not a lonely practice, it is fun when you can share it with your children, partners, family and friends.

This book is written for all you home-bakers out there. It is not a lengthy textbook for professional sourdough bakers, it is for those who want to get back to basics and make bread with the best tools we all have—our very own hands.

We can buy so much 'soul-less' food these days, but there is something soulful about handmade bread. When we make something with our hands at home for those we love, I believe our good feelings and good intentions get transferred into the nourishing food or bread we make—making it taste infinitely better.

This book is a hands-on and highly practical guide to the sourdough bread-making journey. I have been running a successful sourdough bread-making school in Perth for many years now and I have written this book as though I am beside you, guiding you through each step. I have restricted myself from my tendency to over-explain everything, but I have kept those explanations that I feel are necessary for you to understand why certain 'unusual' steps are used.

This book is written from my point of view as a sourdough bread-making teacher and a home-baker. Most of the dough is made by my very own hands, sometimes I make the dough in my home breadmaker or rotary mixer. All breads are baked in my normal home oven, not a commercial oven.

I measure my success by how many people I have 'infected' with my passion and knowledge of sourdough. Every day I receive at least a couple of emails or calls from my students about their sourdough bread-making successes (and problems).

Believe me, your very own bread made with love and your own hands will open many hearts and change many lives! This is the world that I want to open and share with you.

Bread
—the staff of life

We have the ancient Egyptians to thank for the sourdough bread we know today. We have been very lucky to find remnants of sourdough bread that was made over 5000 years ago. The sophisticated ancient Egyptians discovered both bread and beer—they were masters of natural grain fermentation. In fact, the ancient Egyptian word for bread meant 'life', which illustrates the importance of bread in ancient Egyptian life. This ancient bread was shaped as a flat disk, not dissimilar to modern Egyptian pita bread.

It is well known that the first sourdough was discovered accidentally through grain porridge, which has been left for several days. It started to ferment, producing bubbles and a sour smell.

Before modern yeast was discovered in 1680 by French scientist Louis Pasteur, bakers around the world used sour fermented grains as sourdough culture to leaven bread. The oldest sourdough bread known to man was made from emmer wheat, an ancient durum wheat. The ancient Egyptian kept some of the dough to leaven the next day's batches of bread. It is a practice that is still adopted by some traditional bakers in many traditional communities today where yeasts are unavailable or unaffordable.

Sourdough or 'levain' is an intensely alive mass of fermenting flour and water and wild yeast. The wild yeast is from naturally occurring yeast found in whole grains, and in sourdough it is most commonly known as the 'saccharomyces exiguous' yeast. This is the process I use in this book.

It is a slow-acting yeast requiring a long fermentation process. During this process other lactic bacteria, lactobacillus plantarum and lactobacillus brevis, cause a secondary fermentation that creates their own by-products, lactic and acetic acids, and decrease the pH of the dough, creating the characteristic sour flavour of sourdough bread.

The health benefits of sourdough

One of the most important differences between sourdough and other bread is that the sourdough bacteria helps digest all 'phytic acids', a naturally occurring substance in the bran of all wholegrains. This acid inhibits the minerals in the bran to be absorbed by the body. While in straight yeasted breads, about 90 per cent of the phytic acid remains.

Sourdough breads naturally have a low GI (glycaemic index) of 50 or under, about half the GI of yeasted bread. This is due to the acidity of sourdough bread, which slows down the digestion of sugar in the bowel. This explains why you will feel substantially full for longer periods of time when you eat sourdough bread, compared to eating soft, spongy, yeasted commercial bread.

Yeasted bread is made with dough containing 'saccharomyces crevisiae', commercially cultivated yeast, a man-made hybridised strain of saccharomyces yeast. Commercial yeast is fast-acting, strong and aggressive, but it gives a consistent result every time—which is why it is used commercially. Many people have become allergic to commercial yeast.

Sourdough fermentation partly pre-digests gluten, allowing some people who are sensitive to gluten to enjoy eating properly fermented sourdough breads. Please check with your health professional if you are gluten intolerant or allergic to gluten (coeliacs).

A well-known benefit of sourdough fermentation is the complex and flavoursome taste of sourdough bread. It also has a moist crumb with very pleasant 'chewiness'. Properly fermented sourdough bread keeps well for longer—up to 5 days or more—without going dry, stale or mouldy.

Sourdough ingredients

The only ingredients you need to use in making a delicious and nourishing sourdough bread are flour, water and salt. No oil or sugar/honey is required, unless you are making special enriched or flavoured breads.

Flour, being the major ingredient of your bread, is so vital to the taste of your bread. Use the best quality unbleached flour you can afford, preferably organic/biodynamic. Bleaching, apart form its toxicity, destroys (oxidises) beta-carotenoids in the flour, causing the bread you make to be tasteless.

I always endeavour to find biodynamic or organic flours that are grown locally. It is not necessarily true that organic flours always taste better and produce better bread than non-organic counterparts, but for me it is important to look after our precious earth. Locally grown ingredients often mean fresher produce, highly important for wholemeal/wholegrain flours, which can go rancid very fast if not stored properly in a refrigerated or cool room.

Flour

The type of flour you use depends on what type of bread you would like to make. There is no such thing as the best flour, because everyone's taste is so different.

With practice and experimenting you will develop the intuition to 'design' your very own favourite bread. My own preference for everyday bread is a 50/50 wheat and spelt sourdough bread (one being a wholemeal flour) or a 70 per cent unbleached white premium baker's flour and 30 per cent organic wholemeal spelt.

Wheat flour

Wheat flour is the most commonly used flour in bread-making. Wheat flour used in bread-making will have to have gluten (protein) content of more than 10 grams per 100 grams (or 10 per cent of the total weight). Bread made with wheat has good volume and a beautiful sweet, nutty flavour. In Australia, the average gluten content of organic/biodynamic wheat is around 11–12 per cent. Wholemeal flours have more gluten and fibres than white flours.

Spelt flour

Spelt, the ancient wheat, has been heralded lately as a 'better' grain than wheat. Many people who are wheat intolerant have been advised to try spelt as an alternative. There seems to be a common misunderstanding that spelt is somewhat different from wheat. The truth is that spelt is wheat, they belong to the same family of plant, *Triticum*. In Australia, as far as I know, spelt has a higher gluten content than wheat, being around 14 per cent.

Spelt has higher gluten elasticity than wheat and its beautiful tan-brown colour is very appealing. Spelt also has a caramel-like flavour.

Kamut, emmer, einkorn and durum flours

All these grains belong to the same family. However, these are the 'hard wheats' which are commonly known as durum wheat. They are best suited for making pasta. They are to be used sparingly (no more than 25–30 per cent of total flour) in breadmaking because they tend to produce a 'hard and dense' bread, with a thick crust. Kamut, also known as Egyptian Gold, has golden coloured grains and gives a beautiful golden colour in both the crumb and the crust. Semolina flour is made from durum wheat.

Rye, oat and barley flours

These are low-gluten grains. Of the three grains, oat has the least gluten and rye has the most. Rye has another unfavourable quality in bread-making, it contains a polysaccharide, called pentosan, which forms a glue-like substance once it is mixed with water. Because we need water in bread-making, bread made with higher percentage of rye will be dense and heavy, with poor volume. Therefore, these low-gluten flours are to be used sparingly in bread-making (no more than 20 per cent of total flour), unless you specifically want a very dense bread, which is very popular in northern Europe. Rye and oats give a silkiness to any dough, and barley gives the ultimate sweetness. Used sparingly and intelligently, they add complexities and unique flavours and textures to bread.

Water

Always use filtered non-chlorinated, non-flouridated water, especially for your starter culture. Chlorinated water will kill your wild-yeast starter/culture. I have a water filter attached to my kitchen tap, which makes it very simple. Rainwater also makes a beautiful alternative.

The amount of water used, again, depends on the flour used, and the humidity of the room. As a rule, 60 per cent hydration, meaning 600 grams (21oz) of water to 1 kilogram of flour, is a good rule. Start with 600 grams and gradually increase the amount of water if the dough feels dry. Wholemeal flour will require more water due to higher gluten and fibre/bran content. Do not use de-ionised ('dead') water (sold in supermarkets as distilled water). It is usually used for ironing.

Note: It is very important to remember that wet dough makes moist bread, so don't go crazy by adding more flour. If your dough still feels wet after some kneading, never add more flour without a mandatory rest of 20–30 minutes to allow the flour to absorb the water, especially for wholemeal flours.

Salt

Salt enhances the flavour of the bread. Sea-salt, macrobiotic, *fleur de sel* or Celtic salt results in one of the best tasting breads, but you must grind it or dissolve it first. Do not use salt with added 'free-flowing agent' or 'iodine'. My preference is about 20 grams per kilo of flour (2 per cent). You may like to add less, say 1 per cent, it's up to your own taste.

Note: It is important to add salt because:
- Salt controls your fermentation, allowing you to have a long fermentation period.
- Salt increases the strength of the gluten by tightening the gluten structure. A salt-less dough will be slack and sticky and the bread volume will be poor.
- Salt enhances the colour of your crumb and increases its moistness.
- You can reduce the amount of salt to a minimum of 1 per cent. That is about 2 teaspoons of sea salt per kilogram of flour.

A note on baker's percentage

Most commercial bakers use a system of percentages, hence the term 'baker's percentage'. This is something you need to understand to make good sourdough bread.

It starts with the flour. The total weight of the flour in a recipe always equals 100 per cent. The amount of water is anywhere between 60–70 per cent of the flour in most breads (apart from wetter dough bread, such as ciabatta). The amount of salt is about 2 per cent, the amount of starter is 15–30 per cent. So, for example, if you have 1 kilogram (35oz) of flour, you need approximately 600–700 grams (21–24.5oz) of water, 150–300 grams (5–10oz) of starter and 20 grams (0.7oz) of salt.

About grains and gluten

Gluten is the storage protein of wheat or any varieties of wheat (e.g. spelt, emmer, kamut, einkorn). Guten is used as an umbrella term, although technically not correct, to include storage proteins of barley, rye and oats.

Gluten peptides is a term used to describe smaller units of proteins from wheat, barley, rye and oats.

Prolamin is any class of simple amino acid strings high in proline and glutamine. Gliadin and glutenin are the prolamins for wheat, zein for corn, hordein for barley, secalin for rye and avenin for oats.

Gliadin are naturally occurring simple proteins (gluten peptides) found in the gluten of wheat.

Glutenin are also naturally occurring simple proteins (gluten peptides) found in the gluten of wheat.

Types of common wholegrains

Wholegrains containing gluten

Wheat (Triticum aestivum, Triticum vulgare, Triticum dicoccum, Triticum monococcum) is the world's largest cereal grass crop. There are many varieties of wheat, known as the triticums. The whole triticum family contains gluten, including the highly praised spelt. Gluten is the protein storage found in grains. When a person is allergic to gluten, i.e. suffering from coeliac disease, they are allergic to the offending storage proteins (prolamins). In this case, these prolamins are glutenin and gliadin. All wheat and wheat products contain varying amounts of these prolamins.

Other varieties of wheat, often valled 'the ancient wheats' are:

Einkorn (Triticum monoccum) Primitive small-grained wheat of Europe and Asia. Einkorn wheat is represented on some labels as non-glutinous, low-gluten or listed as a corn or maize product.

Emmer (Triticum dicoccum) Another name for durum wheat. Emmer wheat yields glutinous flour used in pastas.

Kamut (Triticum polinicum) Kernels are 2–3 times larger than wheat. Another ancient grain related to durum wheat.

Spelt (Triticum spelta) Another ancient wheat with a mellow nutty flavor.

Low gluten grains

Barley (Hordeum vulgare) Is the world's oldest cultivated crop and more commonly grown in the Middle East/Mediterranean region. Ancient barley varieties naturally shed their husks at harvest. In barley, the offending storage protein (prolamin) is known as hordein. Barley is present in many commercial products, including malt, flavourings, colourings, and/or flavour enhancers.

Oats (Avena sativa) The storage protein (prolamin) is known as avenin. Conflicting studies exist on whether pure oats are problematic for those diagnosed with coeliac disease and dermatitis herpetiformis. Oat prolamins comprise only about 10–15 per cent of the total protein in oats, much less than in wheat, barley or rye.

Rye (Secale cereale) The storage protein in rye is secalin. Rye grain may be fermented to produce alcoholic beverages or industrial alcohol. See Rye Flour on page 20.

Triticale (Triticosecale sp.) (wheat, rye) A hybrid cross of wheat and rye.

Gluten-free wholegrains

Amaranth (Amaranthaceae) Many varieties; related to spinach, beets and pigweed. Tiny seeds are commercially available whole, or ground into a light brown flour with a nutty taste. Highly nutritious. Edible leaves.

Arrowroot (Maranta arundinacea) Herbaceous tropical perennial. The starch, extracted from the rhizomes, is used as a thickener and blends well with gluten-free flours. Interchangeable with cornstarch.

Besan (gram, chickpea flour) Pale yellow flour made from ground, dried chickpeas; very nutritious, high in protein. Used in doughs, dumplings and noodles; as a thickener for sauces; and as a batter for deep-fried food.

Brown rice Kernels of rice from which only the hull has been removed. Cooked brown rice has a slightly chewy texture and a nut-like flavour.

Buckwheat (Fagopyrum esculentum) Herb with triangular-shaped seed and black shell, used whole, cracked or ground into flour.

Cassava (Manihot esculenta) (tapioca, manioc, yuca) Starch, extracted from the root, is ground into flour, which is used as a thickener for soups, fruit fillings and glazes, much like cornstarch.

Corn (Zea mays) Maize, cereal plant native to the Americas. Corn kernels are the largest of cereal seeds. Six major types are dent, flint, flour, sweet, pop and pod corns. Used whole or processed into a multitude of products, including sweeteners, flours and oils.

Glutinous rice The term glutinous refers to its sticky texture when cooked. White, brown or black rice, characterised by broad, short grains that stick together during cooking; mainly used in Asian sweet snacks; also known as sweet rice, sticky rice or waxy rice.

Kudzu Leguminous Asian plant whose roots yield a starchy powdered extract. Used as a thickener. Leaves and stems are also edible.

Millet (Panicum miliaceum) Drought-tolerant grasses with small seeds that can be substituted for sorghum in most recipes.

Potato flour Commercially ground from the whole potato, used as a thickener. Retains potato flavour.

Potato starch flour, potato starch. Commercially prepared from cooked potatoes that are washed of all fibres until only the starch remains.

Quinoa (Chenopodiacum quinoa Willd) Seed of ancient cereal grain of Peru, related to amaranth. Mild nutty flavour. Versatile, can be substituted for any grain. Used whole as a hot cereal; ground into flour. Adds moisture to baked goods.

Rice (Oryza sativa) ('Races' called Indica, Javonica and Sinica) Semi-aquatic member of the grass family. Rice is gluten free and non-allergenic. Categorised as short, medium and long, the edible seed is the staple grain for more than half the world's population.

Sago Starch extracted from tropical palms and processed into flour, meal or pearl sago (similar to tapioca). Used as a thickener.

Xanthan gum is used extensively in almost all commercially produced gluten-free bread flours or breads. Xantham gum is a polysaccharide used as a replacement for the missing gluten, it is an elasticity/viscosity modifier. It is produced by a process involving fermentation of glucose or sucrose from corn by the Xanthomonas campestris bacterium. It adds volume and viscosity to bread and other gluten-free baked goods.

Note: Since xanthan gum is produced by a bacterium that is fed corn to grow, some people allergic to corn will also react to it.

Equipment

The most essential piece of equipment you will need to make good sourdough bread is your hands. This is why in my classes, I teach people how to make bread by hand. Once you have made dough by hand, you will intuitively remember how this dough feels and be able to make perfect sourdough everytime.

However, I will also cover the use of breadmakers, rotary mixers and kitchen aids because some people may have a problem kneading by hand or prefer a faster method of working with a very wet dough, which is almost impossible to knead by hand. However, if it is possible, make sure you make at least five batches of dough by hand first before venturing onto mechanical tools, to develop your 'feel' for dough.

Non-metallic containers and bowls

Due to the acidity of the sourdough, it is important to use a non-metallic container or bowl for both your starter and dough. The pH of a sourdough starter is about 3–4. This is very acidic and it will react with metal utensils. Any glass, ceramic or even a plastic bowl is fine to use.

If find it is easier and less messy to mix the ingredients initially in a bowl with a large spatula.

Digital or electronic scales: Weights and measurements

I believe that bread-making is more of an art than a science. It is about building your intuition rather than mastering precision. However, to train your intuition, and because this book cannot allow you to touch what the dough feels like, you need to start by measuring your ingredients precisely and making your own dough or starter to get it as close possible to what it needs to be.

Therefore, I recommend that all ingredients, including water, are measured in grams using a digital scale. I use the metric system because of the global variability of volume measurements, such as cups or tablespoons/teaspoons, because 500 grams (17oz) is the same anywhere in the world.

The best electronic scale is one that is calibrated to 1 or 2 grams and with a capacity of 5 or 10 kilograms. This is because the weight of your bowl could be already 1 or 2 kilograms when you readjust your scale.

Granite tile

Buying a piece of natural granite stone tile will be the best investment you are ever going to make for your sourdough bread-making. The most effective granite stone tile is 10 millimetres (0.4in) thick and sized to fit your oven. A thicker granite of 20 millimetres will not be effective at all because it will take hours to bring it to a useable temperature for your baking.

Always pre-heat your granite at least 30–45 minutes before baking. This pre-heated granite will give your bread dough a burst of heat, creating an instant oven spring (expansion) and a well-crusted bottom. The even heat will also cook your loaf evenly and thoroughly.

This high searing heat is vital in creating a brown crusty crust and large holes and is especially important in baking pizza and flatbreads such as Turkish and ciabatta, and mimicking artisanal bread baked in wood-fired ovens.

Dough/bench scraper

Those incredibly cheap plastic dough/bench scrapers are another vital and extremely useful tool in your bread-making process. They are very useful in kneading and moving wet dough, cutting your dough and good for cleaning your bench because they will not scratch the surface.

I like to have two each of a couple of different sizes. For example, a small one measuring about 8.5cm x 12cm (3.3 x 4.7in) with a curved edge, and a bigger one 12cm x 21 cm (4.7 x 8.2in). I do not recommend metal scrapers as they will scratch your work surface.

Plant/garden mister

Another very useful tool that is so readily available and very cheap is a pressurised mister. This will moisten the surface of your dough and create a moist environment during baking to give you a crusty and open crust. Always fill the mister with clean filtered water and do not use your mister for any other purpose to avoid contamination/poisoning.

Baker's/pizza peel

For those of you who prefer free-form loaves, I would recommend you buy a sturdy baker's peel or paddle, which are found in most good kitchen shops. I find the aluminium ones with long handles better for handling dough and easier to clean than the wooden paddles.

A baker's peel allows you to transport well-proofed dough to and from your bench to the hot granite surface in your oven with ease and without burning your precious arms or hands.

Baking/parchment paper

A real artisan baker will use a floured baker's peel to transport dough to and from the hot oven. However, for most of us home-bakers, this is not an easy skill to master. Most likely, the dough will end up stuck onto the baker's peel or on the floor.

To overcome this problem, I have taught my students to put the shaped dough onto a piece of baking/parchment paper. This way, transporting the well-formed dough on or off the baker's peel and onto the hot granite surface is effortless.

The baking paper can then be removed from the bread loaf about 15 minutes after baking and can be reused again and again.

Baking/parchment paper is a piece of paper that has been surfaced with silicon. It is non-toxic because silicon is one of the most inert substance known to man. Baking paper is easily available at most grocery stores.

Baking tins

My students often ask me why use baking tins when you can make free-form loaves. There are a few reasons for using tins: One is for making bread for sandwiches, another reason is that free-form loaves have more crust than crumb and my 10-year-old daughter will not eat the crust, therefore wasting most of the bread.

Another practical reason for using baking tins is the ability to bake the bread at your convenience because it can happily rest in the fridge covered with wet cling wrap or inside a large, inflated plastic bag.

The best baking tins are the commercial baking tins made from heavy-gauge aluminised steel alloy and enamelled with silicon. This baking tin requires no oiling or washing because nothing will stick to it. A wipe with a damp soft cloth is all the cleaning it needs after use.

The heavy-gauge steel ensures even and efficient heat absorption and distribution, therefore the sides will brown before the top, ensuring an even cooking of the loaves and crusty brown crusts.

Covering the dough

The best way to keep your dough from drying out while it is rising is to use a container with a lid. If you do not have an enclosed container, another way to cover your dough is by using wet cling wrap because it will stick to almost anything.

Lay the cling wrap over the opening of your bowl, mist the surface of the cling wrap with your water mister, then flip the wrap swiftly over the bowl. The water will ensure the cling wrap sticks to your bowl.

Serrated knife

Although you can buy fancy lame (bakers') knives to slash your loaves, a quality thin-blade, serrated knife does the job well—and it is safer for your fingers. I prefer a Victorinox vegetable peeler or steak knife as the thin blade keeps sharp for years. Most brands will have something similar to this thin-blade serrated knife.

Oven thermometer

Every oven is different, even ones of the same make and model, so know your oven intimately because this is crucial to the success of your bread. Do yourself a big favour and buy an oven thermometer. This is a cheap but very useful tool to know the real temperature of your oven.

There will be 'hot spots' in your oven. To know where hot spots are, lay a piece of baking paper to cover a rack in the middle shelf of your oven and turn your oven on for about 10 minutes at 200°C (390°F). You will see on the 'browned' baking paper, a pattern of where your oven hot spots are. Knowing this, you will know how and where to rotate your bread loaves during baking to get an evenly cooked loaf.

Cooling rack

I use my oven racks to cool my loaves. However, if yours do not suffice, make sure you have a cooling rack so that the freshly baked bread can cool down effectively, allowing air to circulate on the bottom of the loaves.

Bread continues to cook as it cools, so it is important to allow this cooling process to occur naturally before slicing your loaf.

Using machines

Breadmakers

For sourdough bread, do not run the full cycle of your breadmaker. This is because of the slow acting fermentation of sourdough. I only use a breadmaker solely as a kneader.

Breadmakers, in my experience, do a better job at kneading dough than rotary mixers because they create less heat as they knead. However, you must ensure that the often 'built-in' heating element does not kick in at the end of the kneading cycle for automatically rising the dough. Due to lack of 'overheating' compared to rotary mixers, your breadmaker will have a longer life and, at a fraction of the price of a good rotary mixer, it is a far better option for kneading dough.

One feature I do not like is the teflon coating on the bread pan and the dough paddle(s) because teflon, when ingested, is poisonous. Make sure that the teflon surface remains intact on both the pan and the paddles. Replace immediately if it is peeling. Never ever use metal utensils inside your breadmaker pan.

I use the 23-minute 'pasta cycle' on my Sunbeam breadmaker as this allows sufficient time for mixing and kneading the dough without the heating element turning on. I pause the cycle after 5 minutes of mixing to rest the dough. This is an important step because this will allow the gluten in the dough to relax, a process called autolysis, and it allows the flour, especially wholemeal flour, to absorb the water.

I often turn off the cycle halfway as I feel that the dough has had sufficient kneading. Remember, over-kneading will heat up your dough, which in turn means oxidation of the flours, making your bread insipid and flavourless.

It is really important that you do not lose sight of your dough. The adage here is to use your breadmaker as an extension of your hands, so you are still in control of the whole process.

Planetary and spiral mixers

The two most common types of mixer are planetary mixers and spiral mixers. A spiral mixer is a mixer where the bowl moves around a vertical axis and it has a spinning spiral hook. It is superior to the planetary mixer because it does not heat up the dough, even though it kneads the dough faster than a planetary mixer. It is a more expensive mixer than a domestic planetary mixer. Most commercial mixers are spiral mixers. I have seen some smaller (domestic size—the same size as a kitchen aid mixer) spiral mixers from Italy, which are worth searching for.

Most, if not all domestic mixers are planetary mixers, such as a Kitchen Aid and Kenwood Chef. Planetary mixers have a moving head that moves around the stationary bowl. These are multifunctional mixers that can be used to do a variety of tasks, such as beating and mixing cakes.

The downsides to these machines are that they tend to heat up the dough very quickly; they can produce uneven mixing if the dough sticks onto the kneading hook; they can only handle a small amount of dough; and the motor will overheat and wear out fast if you use it too frequently for kneading dough.

One way to overcome overheating (and therefore oxidising your dough) is to use the machine as an extension of your hands, so you are still in control of the whole process. You need to stop your machine for 'resting' the dough often and you need to check your dough frequently to make sure you do not over-knead or overheat your dough.

Remember, heating up your dough means oxidation of the flours, making your bread insipid and flavourless.

Note: Always make sure that you do not overload the machine with too much dough, because this will cause the dough and your mixer to overheat. Follow your mixer manufacturer's instructions and never forget to use your intuitive experience for what the dough should feel like.

Starting from the beginning: Starter culture

The powerhouse or the engine that rises the bread in sourdough bread is the sourdough 'starter' or culture. It is also called *levain* (French), *biga acida* (Italian) or *sauertig* (German). It is simply created by mixing wholegrain/wholemeal flour (preferably organic) with water and leaving it for a few days to ferment. It is the wild yeast that lives just underneath the bran that will self-start the primary fermentation and it is this wild yeast (saccharomyces exiguous) that will rise the dough.

Providing the temperature is cool enough and the fermentation is longer than four hours, a secondary fermentation will occur. It is this lacto-fermentation, created by lactobacilli, not dissimilar to yoghurt, that will give the characteristic sour taste and chewy texture in sourdough bread. Therefore, it is important to allow for longer fermentation, by providing a cooler temperature—25–28°C (77–82°F) is perfect.

The lactobacilli and the wild yeast (in total about 35 microorganisms) work/live together symbiotically to create a pH of 3–4—a very acidic environment that will, in turn, keep other harmful microorganisms away. This is why, providing all the guidelines are met, sourdough starter is practically impossible to kill because nothing else will live in that very acidic environment.

There are basically three types of starter, depending on the flour used. I would strongly recommend that your main starter is made with the best quality organic rye flour. Rye starter is the most robust, less easily contaminated and produces the most flavourful sourdough breads.

Inactive starter

How to start your very own sourdough starter

Creating your own sourdough starter is a very simple process and the characteristic of your starter will be unique to the type of flour used and the surrounding environment. It is easy to create a new starter, but it is not that easy to create a starter that produces desirable characterisitics. Therefore, it is so important to start with the best biodynamic or organic wholegrain flour you can afford.

All you need to do is to mix your wholegrain/wholemeal flour (wheat, spelt or rye) with filtered (chlorine and flouride free) water to create a loose pancake batter. A ratio of 1.25–1.5 water to flour is perfect. Leave to ferment in a warm spot 25–28°C (77–82°F) for 2–3 days until bubbles appear. Then refresh it with more flour and water after bubbles appear every day after. Within a week, you should have a live culture.

Initially, the ratio of water to flour is 1:1.25–1.5 and it is best to start with about 100–150 grams of wholegrain/wholemeal flour. Once your starter is active, try to be as close to a 1:1 flour to water ratio as possible.

When you are creating your sourdough starter, you are basically encouraging the wild yeast, normally occurring in the grains, to grow and create the fermentation. Feeding is a misnomer, it actually means replenishing your starter with more wild yeast, which is in the flour.

The complex and yummy flavour of sourdough is created by slow and long fermentation of the flour in your dough; the starter plays a vital role in the fermentation. If you are going to keep one starter, for the best tasting, well-rounded sourdough bread, I recommend you use a biodynamic/organic whole rye flour or grind your own rye grains.

Right: active starter

Sourdough bread-making methods

The basic steps for making bread are quite simple, all you need is a starter (made from flour and water), flour, water, a little salt, then mix, knead, rise, shape and bake. There are three different methods of making delicious sourdough breads and each method is suited to a different variety of bread. Each method produces unique characteristics so you can be using the same ingredients and create different tasting sourdough breads. Also, different flour works better with a particular method. All of these will be explained under each method.

The Straight method

This is the most common sourdough bread-making method used in this book. This method simply produces the best tasting and textured sourdough loaf, having the most complex flavour and chewiness, characteristic of a well-made artisan sourdough bread. The crumb of this sourdough is full of large uneven holes and the crust has a sweet complex flavour due to the long sourdough fermentation.

This method suits all flours, from white to wholemeal.

Measure ingredients	2–3 mins
Mix ingredients	2–3 mins
Rest	15–20 mins*
Kneading – air kneading	3–5 mins
Rest	30 mins
Final kneading	1–3 mins
First rise (until almost doubled)	4–6 hours or overnight
Shape	5 mins
Second/final rise (until almost doubled)	1–2 hours
Bake	time varies, depending on size of loaf

* Most important for wholegrain/wholemeal dough

The Starter method

I have called this method the starter method because it uses equal weight of starter to flour. Due to the higher proportion of starter used in this method, the bread rises twice as fast, allowing for a better rise/volume but is somewhat slightly lacking in the complexity of flavour and texture.

This method produces a softer, less acidic and a more 'crumbly' texture. If you want to make a soft sandwich loaf, this is the best method to use. This method also is very useful where a higher proportion of wholemeal/wholegrain flours are used because it allows a substantially better rise. It saves the wholemeal sourdough bread from the gluten-tearing property of wholegrain flours. The higher proportion of starter is a lifesaver for mostly rye bread because it negates the glue-like polysaccharide (pentosan) that stops the rye bread from rising.

The crumb of this sourdough bread is soft and dense with more uniform small holes somewhat lacking the airiness of the straight method sourdough loaf. The crust is also softer. It is the best method for producing sandwich sourdough loaves.

The Starter method is suited to all flours, from white to wholemeal, but it lifts wholemeal/wholegrain flour especially when a higher proportion of low-gluten flours, such as rye and barley, are used.

Measure ingredients	2–3 mins
Mix ingredients	2–3 mins
Rest	15–20 mins*
Kneading—air kneading	3–5 mins
Rest	30 mins
Final kneading	1–3 mins
Shape	5 mins
First and final rise	until almost doubled—4–6 hours
Bake	time varies, depending on size of loaf (see baking chart)

*Most important for wholegrain/wholemeal dough

The Dough Retardation method
(or how to fit sourdough into your life)

They say that the best things are born out of necessity. This is one of those. I experimented with the following technique because I had to find ways to make the dough for my classes during my waking hours. My classes start at 10am. In addition, I had to find ways to prolong the fermentation during our scorching Perth summers, where temperatures can reach up to 38°C (100°F) for many days at a time.

This method produces the best-tasting sourdough, coupled with the most convenient method for most people, making it the most versatile of all the three methods.

It is a very simple technique that I would encourage you to take the time to study and master because it will allow you to live your lifestyle undisturbed while being able to make and bake your sourdough at your convenience.

Begin with the Straight method, on page 45, until the first rise.

First rise
- Instead of letting the dough double, let the dough rise until it has increased to one and a quarter (1.25) or one and a half (1.5) times its original size. This will take 1–2 hours, but the key is the size increase, not the time taken.
- Trust your eyes, not the arbitrary time measure.

Second rise
- Now your dough can be stored in the fridge, in a covered container for up to 5 days.
- A slow fermentation will still occur while in the fridge, hence the term 'dough retardation'.

Shape

During the five-day window, whenever you need to make bread:

> Take the dough out of the fridge.
> If you are not using the whole amount, take the quantity of dough you need, and leave the remaining dough in the fridge.
> Immediately, without thawing the dough, shape the dough as desired.

Final rise

- Let the dough rise for the second time until it doubles in volume. This will take longer because the starting dough temperature will be as cold as your fridge temperature.
- You can, if you like, put your dough in a warming oven (about 30–35°C (86–95°F) or in a warm spot for this rise. The use of heat is fine and will not affect the taste of the bread because the dough has had a sufficiently long slow fermentation in the fridge.

Baking

- Bake as per normal.

Measure ingredients	2–3 mins
Mix ingredients	2–3 mins
Rest	15–20 mins*
Kneading—air kneading	3–5 mins
Rest	30 mins
Final kneading	1–3 mins
First rise	short rise—until dough has increased by 25 or 50 per cent time (1–2 hours)
Retardation	in fridge for up to 5 days
Shape	5 mins (**NOTE:** no thawing required)
Second/final rise	until almost doubled, 6 hours or more
Bake	time varies, depending on size of loaf (see baking chart)

Most important for wholegrain/wholemeal dough.

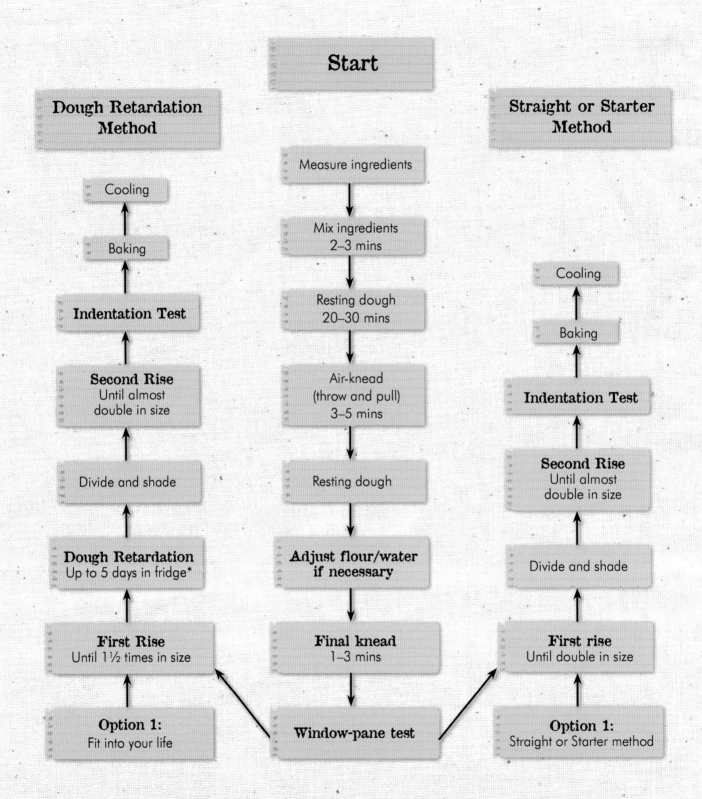

Start

Measure ingredients

Mix ingredients
2–3 mins

Resting dough
20–30 mins

Air-knead
(throw and pull)
3–5 mins

Resting dough

**Adjust flour/water
if necessary**

Final knead
1–3 mins

Window-pane test

**Dough Retardation
Method**

Cooling

Baking

Indentation Test

Second Rise
Until almost
double in size

Divide and shade

Dough Retardation
Up to 5 days in fridge*

First Rise
Until 1½ times in size

Option 1:
Fit into your life

**Straight or Starter
Method**

Cooling

Baking

Indentation Test

Second Rise
Until almost
double in size

Divide and shade

First rise
Until double in size

Option 1:
Straight or Starter method

The sourdough bread-making process

Measure ingredients   **2–3 mins**

- Using preferably a digital scale, weigh all ingredients, including the water. Do not use a measuring jug as this is highly inaccurate.
- Make a habit of measuring your ingredients in this logical order:
    - > Starter
    - > Water
    - > Flour
    - > Salt—over the flour, it must not come into contact with the starter
- Make sure you use non-chlorinated/non-flouridated filtered water and pure sea salt or lake salt (see ingredients).

Mix ingredients   **2–3 mins**

- Using a spatula or a wooden spoon, stir the ingredients together until they form a cohesive mass.

Rest   **15–20 mins**

- The idea behind this method of 'resting' was discovered by Professor Raymond Clavel. He named this process autolyse. Autolyse is the slow speed pre-mixing of the flour and water (excluding all other ingredients), followed by a rest period. Other ingredients are added after the resting period.
- This method will allow you to create a dough that has better volume and superior taste by allowing you to reduce the mixing time, therefore reducing the oxidation of the flours (and thus saving your arms and shoulders), allowing you to create a wetter dough to produce a more open crumb loaf with larger, uneven holes like a ciabatta.
- In my own observation working with sourdough exclusively, it is fine to mix all of the ingredients together: flour, water, starter, salt, prior to the rest/autolyse period. I think this is due to the acidity of sourdough dough.
- This step is most important for wholegrain/wholemeal dough, allowing a greater absorption of water.

Kneading – air kneading   5 mins

- Here, partly due, to a stickier/wetter dough, you may find conventional kneading difficult. The only way to develop the gluten is by literally throwing your dough into the air and then slapping or throwing it onto your work surface.
- It is best to pick up the dough with your fingertips to avoid the dough sticking to your whole hand.
- After you have done this for about 5 minutes, the dough will have developed some elasticity. You may find it easier to oil your work surface and your hands.

Rest   20–30 mins

- As a general rule, 20 minutes rest is sufficient. However, if your dough is still sticky, do a longer rest. This step relaxes the gluten and gives the gluten strands a chance to re-align themselves. Generally a longer rest is required if you are using wholemeal flour because the coarser bran takes longer to absorb the water.
- Your dough should feel soft, elastic and slightly sticky.

Adjust flour or water (if necessary)

- If, after the 30-minute rest period your dough still feels wet or too dry, add more flour or water.
- Add the flour or water by dipping the palm of your hand or fingertips into either the water or flour and then knead it into the dough. Do not add flour or water directly onto the dough because more than often the smallest sprinkling of flour or water is all you need to get the desired consistency.

Final kneading (if necessary)   3–5 mins

- Your dough is ready when it is elastic, soft and looks silky smooth. The colour should also be paler.
- To check whether your dough has had sufficient kneading, you can do a windowpane test by pinching a small amount of dough and then stretching it to create a thin membrane. If your dough can stretch to a thin transparent membrane without tearing, then it is ready.
- Gather your dough together and try to make a ball.

First rise   4–6 hours or overnight

- Let your dough rise until almost doubled. The time taken varies.
- Do not use time as your guide because the time for the dough to double will vary, depending on room temperature, humidity, type of flour used and the activity of your starter.

Shape   5 mins

- Dust your bench generously with semolina flour, invert the dough onto the bench and dust the dough with more semolina flour.
- Using floured hands, shape the dough into a round loaf, scoop the dough onto a baking paper.
- Dust the loaf generously with more semolina flour.

Final rise   2 hours

- Let the dough rise until almost doubled. The time taken will vary.

Bake

- Preheat the oven to 235°C (455°F).
- Bake the dough on the granite tile at the bottom the oven.
- Place a water bath on the top rack.
- Bake for 12–15 minutes until the bottom crust is brown.
- Reduce the oven to 225°C (437°F), move the loaf to a higher rack, bake for a further 20–25 minutes until cooked through.
- The loaf should be brown/golden brown all over and sound hollow when knocked on the bottom.
- If you are unsure whether the loaf has cooked through, turn the oven off and let it sit in the oven for a further 10 minutes.
- Remove the loaf from the oven. Take care not to burn yourself!

Rest

- Let the bread cool on a wire rack before cutting.

Water baths

A water bath is used when baking crusty loaves such as baguettes or ciabatta. To make a water bath, use a shallow baking tray or baking dish. Fill it with boiling water and place it either on the middle or top rack of your oven when baking. It provides hot steam and creates a crusty crust and soft interior crumb. A water bath is not necessary for most sourdough loaves in this book, only use one when specified.

Sourdough tips and tricks

Starter culture

- The most common failure in making sourdough bread is making the dough using a 'dead' or 'inactive' starter. Remember, the starter is the powerhouse of your bread, so if you are using a 'sleepy' starter then your sourdough bread will rise little or not at all, resulting in a 'brick'—flat and hard bread.
- How do you know when your starter is active and ready?
    - > For wheat/spelt starter, i.e. flour to water ratio of 1:1.25–1.5, your starter must look foamy/bubbly.
    - > For rye starter, i.e. flour to water ratio of 1:1, your starter must look sea-sponge/mousse-like with lots of airholes.
    - > Your starter must double in 6–8 hours. After doubling, your starter will collapse—this is the best time to use it because the starter is at its prime because it is 'hungry' for a feed.
- The 'fresh' rule applies for your starter, so once you have an active starter use it. If you are not using it every day, feed it before and after use only.
    - > It may take more than one feed to activate your starter if you have not used it for a while.
    - > You may have to throw out some of your starter if it is strong smelling or if the surface forms a slimy film or a grey water (more information below).
- Keep your starter refrigerated in between making bread if you make bread once a week.
- Do not feed your starter with pre-mix flours of any kind. These pre-mixes often contain commercial yeast, preservatives, emulsifiers and additives that will contaminate/kill your sourdough starter's wild yeasts and lactobacilli in a matter of days.
- For making and feeding starter culture, use organic or biodynamic wholemeal flours and filtered water. This is essential to prevent contamination.
- Your starter will smell between sweet cider and sour vinegar—it must not smell too sour or bad.
- If your starter has a greyish liquid that smells like alcohol or beer and looks 'dead', it is best to throw out the liquid and the top half of the starter. All you need is a tablespoon of your old starter to re-build your starter. Use a new clean container to start again.
- If colourful mould appears (whitish or green is okay), or an unpleasant smell is detected, throw out your starter and sterilise your container before starting again.
- Always keep a back-up starter in the freezer. It will keep in the freezer for up to 6 months or dry your starter in the sun on a sheet of baking paper (spread it thinly). I find drying is better because some bacteria die during freezing.

Note: If you are still having problems with your starter, please feel free to email me at wildsourdough@highway1.com.au or yoke.wildsourdough@gmail.com

Rising

- Most importantly, do not over-rise/overproof your dough during the first and final rise, because over-rising will create a very hard (brick-like) and heavy bread. If you overproof your final rise, the bread may collapse during baking.
- Over-risen dough is slack, tacky/sticky and un-elastic because the gluten has been broken down by the wild yeast and lactobacilli.
- Over-risen dough can be used as the starter for your next batch of sourdough bread, weight per weight. Note: Your next batches of bread will rise faster, so watch carefully.

Baking

- It is better for your digestion to slightly over-bake than under-bake your sourdough.
- Over-baked sourdough bread may be hard/crusty on the outside, but usually still moist in the inside.
- Brown crust tastes better because of the caramelisation of the grain sugars in the crust.
- The wetter the dough, the longer it will take to bake fully.
- The hotter the temperature, the thinner the crust will be. A slow oven will produce a thicker crust.
- Lower your temperature for breads with fruits and sweeteners (apple juice, malt, honey etc.) to avoid burning the crust of the bread before it fully cooks inside.

Baking with commercial bakers' tins

In an oven preheated at 225°C (435°F), standard bakers' tins will take the following times to bake bread:

- A small 340g (11.9oz) commercial tin will hold 800–1000g (28–35oz) of sourdough. It will take approximately 40–45 minutes on 200°C (390°F), and a further 5–10 minutes with the oven off.
- A medium 450g (15.8oz) commercial tin will hold up to 1400g (49oz) of sourdough. It will take 50–60 minutes on 200°C, and a further 15–20 minutes with the oven off.
- A large 680g (24oz) commercial tin will hold up to 1800g (63.5oz) of sourdough. It will take approximately 70–80 minutes on 200°C, and a further 15–25 minutes with the oven off.

Keeping and freezing

- Bread keeps better in a cool, dark place, wrapped in greaseproof paper inside a bread container or a zip-lock bag.
- Do not put bread in the fridge because this will make the bread go stale faster.
- All sourdough bread is suitable for freezing. Zip-lock bags are excellent for storing frozen breads.

Refreshing frozen sourdough bread

- If possible, thaw your frozen bread overnight at room temperature.
- Once thawed, preheat your oven to 200°C for at least half an hour.
- Spray your bread with water using a mister before putting it in the hot oven for 12–15 minutes until it warms through.
- Let the bread cool slightly before slicing.

Slow fermentation and temperature

It is essential that you keep the dough at a cool room temperature of 18–25°C (65–-76°F) and avoid increasing the temperature to speed up the rising of the dough. Slow and long fermentation is essential to create the unique sourdough taste and texture, and more importantly, to allow maximum time for the lactic bacteria to pre-digest grains to make it more nutrient ready.

May your sourdough bread always rise!

Recipes

White sourdough breads

crusty semolina sourdough

I have deliberately put this recipe first in this book because it is one of the easiest to make, providing your starter is fully active. You will be rewarded with the most spectacular loaf, both in taste and look, with the slightest hint of sourdough sourness, a soft interior crumb and a caramel-flavoured crust. This will be one bread you will make again and again.

crusty semolina sourdough

Ingredients

400g (14oz) white starter culture (made with 1:1 ratio of flour to water)

300g (10fl oz) filtered water, room temperature

350g (12oz) unbleached white wheat flour (premium baker's flour)

200g (7oz) fine semolina flour

3 teaspoons (15g) sea salt, finely ground

Extra semolina flour for dusting

1265g (45oz) makes one large or two small free-form loaves

Method

Measure ingredients

- Using, preferably, a digital scale, weigh all ingredients, including the water. Put all ingredients in a non-metallic bowl, starting with water and starter, flour and then salt last.

Mix ingredients   2–3 mins

- Using a spatula or wooden spoon, stir the ingredients together until they form a cohesive mass.

Rest   30 mins

- Rest the dough in the bowl for 30 minutes. This step allows the semolina flour to absorb the water.

Kneading—air kneading   5 mins

- This dough is wet and you may find it easier to oil the work surface or bench and your hands.
- Using your fingertips, throw the dough into the air and then slap/throw it onto the bench.
- Repeat this action for about 5 minutes until the dough develops some elasticity.

Rest   20–30 mins

- Rest the dough for another 30 minutes. This relaxes the gluten and gives the gluten strands a chance to re-align themselves.
- Your dough should feel soft, elastic and slightly sticky.

Adjust flour or water (if necessary)

- If, after the 30-minute rest period, your dough still feels wet or too dry, add a small amount of water or flour. I find the best way to do this is to dip your hands in the water or flour and re-knead the dough until it feels right.

Final kneading (if necessary) 3–5 mins

- If the dough isn't elastic, soft and looking silky smooth, air knead further.
- Do a windowpane test.

Shape   5 mins

- Dust your bench generously with semolina flour, invert the dough onto the bench and dust the dough with more semolina flour.
- Using floured hands, shape the dough into a round loaf and scoop the dough onto baking paper.
- Dust the loaf generously with more semolina flour.

Final rise   4 hrs

- Let the dough rise until doubled—the time taken will vary—don't be alarmed though, the dough will look flat as it increases in size.
- You may see a crack on the surface of the dough. This is a sign that it is almost ready.
- Do an indentation test.

Bake

- Preheat oven to 235°C (455°F).
- Place the granite tile in the bottom of the oven to heat up. This may take up to 30 minutes.
- Place the dough on the granite in the bottom of the oven with a water bath on the top rack. Cook for 12–15 minutes until the bottom crust is brown.
- Reduce the oven to 225°C (437°F), move the loaf to a higher rack and bake for a further 20–25 minutes until cooked through.
- The loaf should be brown/golden brown all over and sound hollow when knocked on the bottom.
- If you are unsure whether the loaf has cooked through, turn the oven off and let it sit in the oven for a further 10 minutes.
- Remove the loaf from the oven, taking care not to burn yourself!

Rest

- Let the bread cool on a rack before cutting.

Bread is suitable for freezing and will keep for a couple of months frozen.

pain au levain

This is an easy but delicious bread for your first attempt. It will be easy to mix and knead, giving you a moist chewy loaf with a delicious crust. This is quite different bread to the crusty semolina. The more acidic rye starter and the double fermentation (first and second rises) give this loaf a more complex flavour and a silkier, moister and chewier crumb.

pain au levain

Ingredients

150g (5oz) rye starter culture
(made with 1:1.5 flour to water ratio)

600g (22oz) unbleached white
premium bakers flour

360g (13fl oz) filtered water,
room temperature

2 teaspoons (10g) sea salt,
finely ground

1142g (40oz) makes one
or two free-form loaves

Method

Measure ingredients

- Using preferably a digital scale, weigh all ingredients, including the water. Put all ingredients in a non-metallic bowl, starting with water and starter, flour and salt last.

Mix ingredients   2–3 mins

- Using a spatula or wooden spoon, stir the ingredients together until they form a cohesive mass.

Rest   15–20 mins

- Rest the dough in the bowl for 15–20 minutes. This step is most important for wholegrain/wholemeal dough, allowing a greater absorption of water.

Kneading—air kneading   5 mins

- Using your fingertips, throw the dough into the air and then slap/throw it onto the bench.
- Repeat this action for about 5 minutes, until the dough develops some elasticity. You may find it easier to oil your bench and your hands.

Rest   20–30 mins

- Rest the dough for another 20 minutes. As a general rule, 20 minutes rest is sufficient, however, if your dough is still sticky, rest it for longer. This relaxes the gluten and gives the gluten strands a chance to re-align themselves.
- Your dough should feel soft, elastic and slightly sticky.

Adjust flour or water (if necessary)

- If after the 30-minute rest period your dough still feels wet or too dry, add more water or flour. I find the best way to do this is to dip your hands in the water or flour and re-knead the dough until it feels right.

Final kneading (if necessary)   3–5 mins

- If the dough isn't elastic, soft and looks silky smooth, air knead further.
- Do a windowpane test.
- Gather your dough into a ball shape. Let it rest in a non-metallic container or bowl covered with a wet tea towel or cling wrap.

First rise   4–6 hours

- Let your dough rise until it has almost doubled—the time taken will vary.

Divide and shape   5 mins

- Divide the dough into 2 x 600g (22oz) pieces or leave as one loaf. Shape the loaves as desired.
- Gently slip the dough onto baking paper.

Second/final rise   2 hours

- Rise again until the dough is almost doubled—about 2 hours at a comfortable room temperature of around 20–25°C (68°F–77°F). Make sure the dough is covered or mist it with water to prevent drying.

Bake

- Preheat oven to 235°C (455°F).
- Bake in the oven for about 10 minutes, then reduce the oven to 225°C (437°F) for a further 15–20 minutes for the 600g loaves, or longer for a larger loaf.
- The loaves should be brown/golden brown all over and sound hollow when knocked on the bottom.
- If you are unsure whether the loaf has cooked through, turn the oven off and let it sit in the oven for a further 10 minutes.
- Remove the loaves from the oven, taking care not to burn yourself!

Rest

- Let the bread cool on a rack before cutting.

Bread is suitable for freezing and will keep for a couple of months frozen.

sourdough sandwich loaf

This is the answer to the ubiquitous white supermarket sandwich bread but, being sourdough, it is a healthier version of what most people know as bread. This method will yield a fluffier, softer, somewhat less chewy bread than your normal sourdough. The sourdough flavour will be milder and less acidic.

Ingredients

500g (18oz) white spelt/wheat starter active (made with 1:1 ratio of flour to water)

650g (23oz) unbleached white spelt or wheat flour

350g (12fl oz) filtered water

3 teaspoons (15g) sea salt, finely ground

1515g (53 oz) makes one sandwich loaf

Method

Measure ingredients

- Using, preferably, a digital scale, weigh all ingredients, including the water, and put them in a non-metallic bowl, starting with water and starter, flour and then salt last.

Mix ingredients   2–3 mins

- Using a spatula or wooden spoon, stir the ingredients together until they form a cohesive mass.

Rest   15–20 mins

- Rest the dough in the bowl for 15–20 minutes. This step allows the flour to absorb the water.

Kneading—air kneading   5 mins

- This dough is wet and you may find it easier to oil the work surface or bench and your hands.
- Using your fingertips, throw the dough into the air and then slap/throw it onto the bench.
- Repeat this action for about 5 minutes until the dough develops some elasticity.

Rest   20–30 mins

- Rest the dough in the bowl for 30 minutes. As a general rule, 20 minutes rest is sufficient. However, if your dough is still sticky, do a longer rise—this step relaxes the gluten and gives the gluten strands a chance to re-align themselves.
- Your dough should feel soft, elastic and slightly sticky.

Adjust flour or water (if necessary)

- If after the 30-minute rest period your dough still feels wet or too dry, add more water or flour. I find the best way to do this is to dip your hands in the water or flour and re-knead the dough until it feels right.

Final kneading (if necessary)   3–5 mins

- If the dough isn't elastic, soft and looks silky smooth, air knead further.
- Do a windowpane test.

Shape   5 mins

- Shape the dough into a ball, let it rest for about 20 minutes to relax the gluten.
- Stretch the dough to a rectangle 20 x 25cm (8 x 10in).
- Roll tightly, as though you were rolling a Swiss roll, close the seam well by pressing the edges together.
- Gently lift the roll into your tin, then roll it around inside the tin to fit it evenly.
- Mist the surface of the dough with water, then sprinkle with seeds if you wish.

First and final rise   4–6 hours

- Let the dough rise until it is almost doubled—the time taken will vary.

Bake

- Preheat oven to 235°C (455°F).
- Bake for about 15 minutes, then reduce the oven to 215°C (419°F) for a further 30–40 minutes until the bread is cooked through. Time taken for baking will vary.
- The loaves should be brown/golden brown all over and sound hollow when knocked on the bottom.
- Remove the tin from the oven, immediately invert loaf onto a cooling rack, taking care not to burn yourself!
- If you are unsure whether the loaf has cooked through, turn the oven off and let it sit in the oven for a further 10 minutes.

Rest

- Let the bread cool on a rack before cutting.

Bread is suitable for freezing and will keep
for a couple of months frozen.

sourdough pain de mie
—sourdough milk bread
(dairy or dairy free)

This recipe requires one extra step, which is to make a milk/soy milk starter. Milk/soy milk will give you a softer and moister crumb, reminiscent of a store-bought commercial sandwich loaf. It is a tasty, nutritious and soft sandwich bread.

Ingredients

Step 1: Liquid starter
50g (2oz) rye starter culture (made with 1:1.5 ratio of flour to water)

250g (9oz) unbleached white spelt or wheat flour

500g (18fl oz) Whole milk or fermented soy milk or rice milk

Stir ingredients well.

This will yield 800g (29fl oz) milk starter

Let the starter ferment overnight at room temperature until it has risen and is active and bubbly.

Step 2: Dough
800ml (27fl oz) liquid starter

600g (21oz) unbleached white wheat/spelt or atta flour

3 teaspoons (15g) sea salt, finely ground

1415g (50oz) makes one large sandwich loaf

Method

Measure ingredients
- Using, preferably, a digital scale, weigh all ingredients, including the water. Put all the ingredients in a non-metallic bowl, starting with all of the milk starter, flour and then salt last.

Mix ingredients   2–3 mins
- Using a spatula or wooden spoon, stir the ingredients together until they form a cohesive mass.

Rest   15–20 mins
- Rest the dough in the bowl for 15–20 minutes. This step allows the flour to absorb the water.

Kneading—air kneading   5 mins
- This dough is wet and you may find it easier to oil the work surface or bench and your hands.
- Using your fingertips, throw the dough into the air and then slap/throw it onto the bench.
- Repeat this action for about 5 minutes until the dough develops some elasticity.

Rest   20–30 mins
- As a general rule, 20 minutes rest is sufficient. However, if your dough is still sticky, rest for longer—this step relaxes the gluten and gives the gluten strands a chance to re-align themselves.
- Your dough should feel soft, elastic and slightly sticky.

Adjust flour or water (if necessary)

- If after the 30-minute rest period your dough still feels wet or too dry, add more water or flour. I find the best way to do this is to dip your hands in the water or flour and re-knead the dough until it feels right.

Final kneading (if required)   3–5 mins

- If the dough isn't elastic, soft and looking silky smooth, air knead further.
- Do a windowpane test.

Shape   5 mins

- Shape the dough into a ball and let it rest for about 20 minutes to relax the gluten.
- Stretch the dough to a rectangle of 20 x 25cm (8 x 10 inches).
- Roll tightly as though you were rolling a Swiss roll, close the seam well by pressing the edges together.
- Gently lift the roll into your tin, then roll it around inside the tin to fit it evenly.
- Mist the surface of the dough with water, then sprinkle with seeds if you wish.

First and final rise   4–6 hours

- Let the dough rise until it is almost doubled in size—the time taken will vary.

Bake

- Preheat oven to 235°C (455°F).
- Bake the dough for about 10 minutes, then reduce the oven to 215°C (419°F) for a further 30–40 minutes. Time for baking will vary.
- The loaves should be brown/golden brown all over and sound hollow when knocked on the bottom.
- Remove the tin from the oven, immediately invert the loaf onto a cooling rack, taking care not to burn yourself.
- If you are unsure whether the loaf has cooked through, turn the oven off and let it sit in the oven for a further 10 minutes.

Rest

- Let the bread cool on a rack before cutting.

Bread is suitable for freezing and will keep for a couple of months frozen.

polenta/corn bread
(Portuguese broa)

This bread was created for one of my dearest friends, Emmanuella, who was born in Portugal. I had never tasted an authentic Portuguese broa. I only had a description from her. When I finally succeeded in making this loaf after a couple of tries, Emmanuella said it brought back memories of her Portuguese family and cured her homesickness.

Don't be alarmed at the flattening (spreading) of the dough as it rises, this dough will spring to an unbelievable volume (about 30 per cent oven spring will occur) and it will form cracks all over its surface, creating a very dramatic looking, rustic loaf indeed.

Note: *Corn is one of the most genetically modified (GM) crops. Please take the time and effort to look for organic/biodynamic polenta, which by definition should be GM free.*

polenta/corn bread (Portuguese broa)

Ingredients

400g (14oz) white starter culture (made with 1:1 ratio of flour to water)

250g (8.8fl oz) filtered water, room temperature

50g (1.7oz) coarse polenta

150g (5.3oz) fine polenta

300g (11oz) unbleached white wheat flour

3 teaspoons (15g) sea salt, finely ground

Extra polenta for dusting

1115g (40 oz) makes one large free-form loaf

Method

Measure ingredients

- Using, preferably, a digital scale, weigh all ingredients, including the water. Put all ingredients in a non-metallic bowl, starting with water and starter, flour and then salt last.

Mix ingredients   2–3 mins

- Using a spatula or wooden spoon, stir the ingredients together until they form a cohesive mass.

Rest   15–20 mins

- Rest the dough in the bowl for 15–20 minutes. This step allows the flour to absorb the water.

Kneading—air kneading   5 mins

- This dough is wet and you may find it easier to oil the work surface or bench and your hands.
- Using your fingertips, throw the dough into the air and then slap/throw it onto the bench.
- Repeat this action for about 5 minutes until the dough develops some elasticity.

Rest   20–30 mins

- As a general rule, 20 minutes rest is sufficient. However, if your dough is still sticky, rest it for longer. This step relaxes the gluten and gives the gluten strands a chance to re-align themselves.
- Your dough should feel soft, elastic and slightly sticky.

Adjust flour or water (if necessary)

- If after the 30-minute rest period your dough still feels wet or too dry, add more water or flour. I find the best way to do this is to dip your hands in the water or flour and re-knead the dough until it feels right.

Shape   5 mins

- Dust your bench generously with polenta, invert the dough onto the bench and dust the dough with more polenta.
- Using floured hands, shape the dough into a round loaf, scoop the dough onto baking paper.
- Dust the loaf generously with more polenta.

Final rise   4–6 hours

- Let the dough rise until doubled—don't be alarmed, the dough will flatten as it increases in size.
- You may see a crack on the surface of the dough, this is a sign that it is almost ready.
- Do an indentation test.

Bake

- Preheat oven to 235°C (455°F).
- Place the granite tile in the bottom of the oven to heat up. This may take up to 30 minutes.
- Place the dough on the granite in the bottom of the oven with a water bath on the top rack. Cook for 10–12 minutes until the bottom crust is brown.
- Reduce the oven to 225°C (437°F), remove the water bath, move the loaf to a higher rack and bake for a further 25–30 minutes until cooked through.
- The loaf should be brown/golden brown all over and sound hollow when knocked on the bottom.
- If you are unsure whether the loaf has cooked through, turn the oven off and let it sit in the oven for a further 10 minutes.
- Remove the loaf from the oven, taking care not to burn yourself!

Rest

- Let the bread cool on a rack before cutting.

Bread is suitable for freezing and will keep for a couple of months frozen.

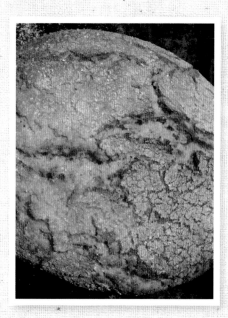

Wheat grain sourdough breads

Here are some general tips and tricks for making 100 per cent wholegrain sourdough bread.

- To create lightness:
    - > Use more starter—about 50 per cent of the total flour weight— to increase wild yeast and lactobacillus fermentation.
    - > Use a 'high gluten' wheat/spelt starter instead of a rye starter.
- A wetter than normal dough results in a better textured bread with a moist crumb.
- Do one rise only—because most wholemeal dough, especially those with a substantial amount of low gluten (rye, barley, oat) or gluten-free flour (corn/polenta, rice, millet)—will not rise a second time.
- A hotter oven, initially preheated to 250°C (480°F), creates oven-spring.
- A hot water bath creates a steamy environment in the oven and prevents drying out of the crust while cooking the interior crumb. It also helps to create a beautiful thick crackling crust (see page 53).

wholemeal sourdough sandwich bread

When you eat yeasted wholemeal or wholegrain bread that has been made quickly—most commercial bread is made and baked within 90 minutes from flour to bread—your body is getting the starches, sugars and fibres, but completely missing the minerals and vitamins contained in the grains.

This is because all wholegrains contain phytic acids or phytates, a naturally occuring substance in grains. Sourdough fermentation eliminates most if not all phytates, allowing your body to absorb the nutrients and vitamins.

Ingredients

500g (18oz) whole-spelt/wheat starter (made with 1:1 flour to water ratio)

350g (12fl oz) filtered water

650g (23oz) whole-spelt or whole-wheat flour

3 teaspoons (15g) sea salt, finely ground

1515g (53oz) makes one sandwich loaf

Method

Measure ingredients

- Using, preferably, a digital scale, weigh all ingredients, including the water. Put all ingredients in a non-metallic bowl, starting with water and starter, flour and then salt last.

Mix ingredients   2–3 mins

- Using a spatula or wooden spoon, stir the ingredients together until they form a cohesive mass.

Rest   15–20 mins

- Rest the dough in the bowl for 15–20 minutes. This step allows the flour to absorb the water.

Kneading—air kneading   5 mins

- This dough is wet and you may find it easier to oil the work surface or bench and your hands.
- Using your fingertips, throw the dough into the air and then slap/throw it onto the bench. Repeat this action for about 5 minutes until the dough develops some elasticity.

Rest   20–30 mins

- Rest the dough for another 20 minutes. As a general rule, 20 minutes rest is sufficient. However, if the dough is still sticky, rest for longer. This relaxes the gluten and gives the gluten strands a chance to re-align themselves.
- The dough should feel soft, elastic and slightly sticky.

Adjust flour or water (if necessary)

- If after the 30-minute rest period the dough still feels wet or too dry, add more water or flour. I find the best way to do this is to dip your hands in the water or flour and re-knead the dough until it feels right.

Final kneading (if necessary)   3–5 mins

- If the dough isn't elastic, soft and looks silky, air knead further.
- Do a windowpane test.

Shape   5 mins

- Shape the dough into a ball, let it rest for about 20 minutes to relax the gluten.
- Stretch the dough to a rectangle 20 x 25cm (8 x 10in).
- Roll tightly as though you were rolling a Swiss roll and close the seam well by pressing the edges together.
- Gently lift the roll into the tin, then roll it around inside the tin to fit it evenly.
- Mist the surface of the dough with water, then sprinkle with seeds if you wish.

First and final rise   4–6 hours

- Let the dough rise until almost doubled—the time taken will vary.

Bake

- Preheat oven to 235°C (455°F).
- Bake in the over for 12–15 minutes, then reduce the oven to 215°C (419°F) for a further 30–40 minutes. Time for baking will vary.
- Remove the tin from he oven, immediately invert loaf onto a cooling rack, taking care not to burn yourself!
- If you are unsure whether the loaf has cooked through, turn the oven off and let the loaf sit in the oven for a further 10 minutes.

Rest

- Let the bread cool on a rack before cutting.

Bread is suitable for freezing and will keep for a couple of months frozen.

multigrain sourdough bread

This 'soaking' and/or soaking and cooking methods are the best methods to incorporate whole grains or seeds into sourdough breads. Soaking liquid can be filtered water with an acidulant, such as natural yoghurt/kefir whey (the best) or a squeeze of lemon.

It is worth noting, that almost all commercial multigrain bread (sourdough or yeasted) is made with white baker's flour (wheat). The healthy appearance is created by the addition of multigrains/seeds. In my view, the best multigrain breads are made with 50 per cent unbleached white baker's flour and 50 per cent coarsely milled wholemeal flours—and can be either wheat or spelt.

multigrain sourdough bread

Ingredients

200g (7oz) whole wheat/spelt starter (made with 1:1 flour to water ratio)

400g (14fl oz) filtered water

400g (14oz) wholegrain spelt/wheat flour

500g (18 oz) unbleached white spelt or wheat flour

300g (11oz) soaked grains and/or seeds (fresh and roughly crushed, especially flaxseed, to release nutrients). Soak grains overnight or at least 6 hours in 300g of water

4 teaspoons (20g) sea salt

Extra wholegrain flour for dusting

1820g (64oz) makes three free-form loaves or two small sandwich loaves (340gm bread tin)

Notes on soaking grains

- Depending on the types of grains/ seeds used, you may need an extra 50g of water to moisten the grains/seeds.
- The final dough must not feel dry.

Method

Measure ingredients

- Using, preferably, a digital scale, weigh all ingredients, including the water. Put all ingredients in a non-metallic bowl, starting with water and starter, flour and then salt last.

Mix ingredients   2–3 mins

- Using a spatula or wooden spoon, stir the ingredients together until they form a cohesive mass.

Rest   15–20 mins

- Rest the dough in the bowl for 15–20 minutes. This step allows the flour to absorb the water.

Kneading—air kneading   5 mins

- This dough is wet and you may find it easier to oil the work surface or bench and your hands.
- Using your fingertips, throw the dough into the air and then slap/throw it onto the bench.
- Repeat this action for about 5 minutes until the dough develops some elasticity.

Rest   20–30 mins

- Rest the dough for 20 minutes. As a general rule, 20-minutes rest is sufficient. However, if the dough is still sticky, rest for longer. This step relaxes the gluten and gives the gluten strands a chance to re-align themselves.
- The dough should feel soft, elastic and slightly sticky.
- Do a windowpane test.

Adding multigrain and seeds

- Dust the bench with some wholemeal flour, add the soaked grains/seeds and mix well.

Rest   30 mins

- Rest the dough for another 30 minutes. This is a vital step for this loaf as the grain/seeds will continue to absorb water. The final dough must not feel dry.

Adjust flour or water (if necessary)

- If after the 30-minute rest period the dough still feels too wet or dry, add more water or flour. I find the best way to do this is to dip your hands in the water or flour and re-knead the dough until it feels right.

Divide and shape   5 mins

- Divide the dough into two for sandwich loaves, or three for free-form loaves. Shape each dough portion into a ball, let it rest for about 20 minutes to relax the gluten.
- Stretch the dough to a rectangle of 20 x 25cm (8 x 10in).
- Roll tightly as though you were rolling a Swiss roll, close the seam well by pressing the edges together.
- Gently lift the roll into the tin for sandwich bread then roll it around inside the tin to fit it evenly.
- For free-form loaves, place the dough onto baking paper.
- Mist the surface of the dough with water, then sprinkle with more grains/seeds if you wish.

First and final rise   4–6 hours

- Let the dough rise until almost doubled—the time taken will vary.

Bake

- Preheat oven to 235°C (455°F).
- For sandwich loaves, bake for about 10 minutes, then reduce the oven to 210°C (410°F) for a further 25–30 minutes.
- For free-form loaves, bake for about 10 minutes, then reduce the oven to 210°C (410°F) for a further 20–25 minutes.
- Remove the tin from the oven, immediately invert loaf onto a cooling rack, taking care not to burn yourself!
- If you are unsure whether the loaves have cooked through, turn the oven off and let the loaves sit in the oven for a further 10 minutes.

Rest

- Let the bread cool on a rack before cutting.

Bread is suitable for freezing and will keep for a couple of months frozen.

black rice sourdough ciabatta

This is one of my favourite sourdough breads, and it is very simple to make. I first tasted a black rice bread (it was yeasted, not sourdough) in Ubud, Bali, and absolutely loved its almost molasses-like complex flavour and fragrance. Here, scalded and cooked black rice is added to basic sourdough bread, resulting in one of the most dramatic looking sourdough breads. This one is a must-try for everyone!

I recommend using spelt instead of wheat in this recipe, the caramel flavour of spelt marries well and enhances the unique flavour of black rice.

How to cook the black rice:

- 1 cup black rice, washed and scalded with 3 cups of boiling hot water, then left overnight to soak.
- Throw away soaking water, rinse well, and drain thoroughly.
- Use 2–3 cups filtered water to cook the rice by the absorption method.
- Bring rice and water to the boil, reduce heat and simmer for 20–30 minutes with the lid on.
- Cool before using.

black rice sourdough ciabatta

Ingredients

200g (7oz) whole wheat/spelt starter (made with 1:1 flour to water ratio)

500g (18fl oz) water

450g (16oz) wholemeal spelt/wheat flour

450g (16oz) unbleached white spelt/wheat flour

300g (11oz) cooked black rice

4 teaspoons (20g) sea salt

Extra wholemeal flour for dusting

1920g (68oz) makes three free-form loaves

Method

Measure ingredients

- Using, preferably, a digital scale, weigh all ingredients, including the water. Put all ingredients in a non-metallic bowl, starting with water and starter, flour and then salt last.

Mix ingredients · · · · · · · 2–3 mins

- Using a spatula or wooden spoon, stir the ingredients together until they form a cohesive mass.

Rest · · · · · · · 15–20 mins

- Rest the dough in the bowl for 15–20 minutes. This step allows the flour to absorb the water.

Kneading—air kneading · · · 5 mins

- This dough is wet and you may find it easier to oil the work surface or bench and your hands.
- Using your fingertips, throw the dough into the air and then slap/throw it onto the bench.
- Repeat this action for about 5 minutes until the dough develops some elasticity.

Rest · · · · · · · 20–30 mins

- Rest the dough for another 20 minutes. As a general rule, 20 minutes rest is sufficient. However, if the dough is still sticky, rest it for longer. This step relaxes the gluten and gives the gluten strands a chance to re-align themselves.
- The dough should feel soft, elastic and slightly sticky.
- Do a windowpane test.

Add the black rice

- Dust the bench with wholemeal flour, add the cooked and cooled black rice and mix well.

- Rest for about 30 minutes. If after the 30-minute rest period the dough still feels wet or too dry, add more flour or water. I find the best way to do this is to dip your hands into the flour or water and re-knead until it feels right.
- Adjust flour or water, if necessary.

Shape   5 mins
- Divide the dough into three portions. Shape each dough portions into a ball, let it rest for about 20 minutes to relax the gluten.
- Stretch the dough to a rectangle 20 x 25cm (8 x 10in).
- Roll tightly as though you were rolling a Swiss roll, close the seam well by pressing the edges together.
- Gently place onto baking paper.
- Mist the surface of the dough with water.

First and final rise   4–6 hours
- Let the dough rise until almost doubled—the time taken will vary.

Bake
- Preheat oven to 235°C (455°F) for at least 30 minutes.
- Prepare a water bath in a shallow oven tray.
- Bake for about 10 minutes, then reduce the oven to 210°C (410°F) for a further 20–25 minutes.
- Time for baking will vary.
- Remove the loaves from the oven, immediately invert loaves onto a cooling rack, taking care not to burn yourself.
- If you are unsure whether the loaves have cooked through, turn the oven off and let the loaves sit in the oven for a further 10 minutes.

Rest
- Let the bread cool on a rack before cutting.

Bread is suitable for freezing and will keep for a couple of months frozen.

quinoa spelt sourdough

Cooked quinoa gives this bread a silky texture and nutty flavour. It is a truly
beautiful and delicious bread, well worth the extra step of cooking quinoa.
Soaking and cooking the quinoa, then fermenting it in the bread, makes it more
readily digestible and absorbed by our bodies. You can use leftover cooked
quinoa or frekkeh (cracked green wheat). Red quinoa gives this
sourdough bread an extra dramatic look!

Quinoa, like all whole grains, requires an overnight soaking to remove saponin
(soap-like naturally occuring substance) and phytates.

It is worth noting that by adding quinoa, it increases the protein and fibre
content of the sourdough and lowers the glycaemic index (GI),
making it highly desirable for those who want to lose weight.

quinoa spelt sourdough

Ingredients

200g (7oz) whole-spelt starter
(made with 1:1 flour to water ratio)

500g (17 fl oz) water

250g (9oz) soaked and cooked
quinoa (cooled)

350g (12oz) unbleached white
spelt/wheat flour

400g (14oz) wholegrain spelt flour

4 teaspoons (20g) sea salt

1720g (61oz) makes three
free-form loaves

Method

Measure ingredients

- Using, preferably, a digital scale, weigh all ingredients, including the water. Put all ingredients in a non-metallic bowl, starting with water and starter, flour and then salt last.

Mix ingredients   2–3 mins

- Using a spatula or wooden spoon, stir the ingredients together until they form a cohesive mass.

Rest   15–20 mins

- Rest the dough in the bowl for 15–20 minutes. This step allows the flour to absorb the water.

Kneading—air kneading   5 mins

- This dough is wet and you may find it easier to oil the work surface or bench and your hands.
- Using your fingertips, throw the dough into the air and then slap/throw it onto the bench.
- Repeat this action for about 5 minutes until the dough develops some elasticity.

Rest   20–30 mins

- Rest the dough for 20 minutes. As a general rule, 20 minutes rest is sufficient. However, if the dough is still sticky, rest it for longer. This step relaxes the gluten and gives the gluten strands a chance to re-align themselves.
- The dough should feel soft, elastic and slightly sticky.
- Do a windowpane test.

Add the quinoa

- Dust the bench with some wholemeal flour, add the cooked and cooled quinoa and mix well.
- Rest for about 30 minutes. If after the 30 minutes rest period the dough still feels wet or too dry, add more flour or water. I find the best way to do this is to dip your hands in the water or flour and re-knead the dough until it feels right.

Shape   5 mins

- Divide the dough into three portions. Shape each dough portion into a ball, let it rest for about 20 minutes to relax the gluten.
- Stretch the dough to a rectangle of 20 x 25cm (8 x 10in).
- Roll tightly as though you were rolling a Swiss roll, close the seam well by pressing the edges together.
- Gently place onto baking paper.
- Mist the surface of the dough with water

First and final rise   4–6 hours

- Let the dough rise until almost doubled—the time taken will vary.

Bake

- Preheat oven to 235°C (455°F) for at least 30 minutes. Prepare a water bath in a shallow oven tray and place in the oven.
- Bake for about 10 minutes, then reduce the oven to 210°C (410°F) for a further 20–25 minutes.
- Time for baking will vary.
- Remove the loaves from the oven and immediately invert onto a cooling rack, taking care not to burn yourself!
- If you are unsure whether the loaves have cooked through, turn the oven off and let it sit in the oven for a further 10 minutes.

Rest

- Let the bread cool before cutting.

Bread is suitable for freezing and will keep for a couple of months frozen.

millet sourdough

I love the smell and flavour of cooked millet. This is one of those breads that looks and feels good enough to eat. If you use wheat flour, this bread will have an attractive golden yellow colour. The flavour is nutty and sweet.

It's worth noting that by adding millet, the protein and fibre content of the sourdough is increased and it lowers the glycaemic index (GI), making it highly desirable for those who want to lose weight.

Ingredients

200g (7oz) whole-spelt starter or whole-wheat (made with 1:1 flour to water ratio)

500g (17fl oz) water

250g (9oz) soaked and cooked hulled millet (cooled)

350g (12oz) unbleached white spelt/wheat flour

400g (14oz) wholemeal spelt flour or whole-wheat flour

4 teaspoons (20g) sea salt

Extra wholemeal flour for dusting

1720g (61oz) makes three free-form loaves

Method

Measure ingredients

- Using, preferably, a digital scale, weigh all ingredients, including the water. Put all ingredients in a non-metallic bowl, starting with water and starter, flour and then salt last.

Mix ingredients   2–3 mins

- Using a spatula or wooden spoon, stir the ingredients together until they form a cohesive mass.

Rest   15–20 mins

- Rest the dough in the bowl for 15–20 minutes. This step allows the flour to absorb the water.

Kneading—air kneading   5 mins

- This dough is wet and you may find it easier to oil the work surface or bench and your hands.
- Using your fingertips, throw the dough into the air and then slap/throw it onto the bench.
- Repeat this action for about 5 minutes until the dough develops some elasticity.

Rest   20–30 mins

- Rest the dough. As a general rule, 20 minutes rest is sufficient. However, if the dough is still sticky, rest it for longer. This step relaxes the gluten and gives the gluten strands a chance to re-align themselves.
- The dough should feel soft, elastic and slightly sticky.
- Do a windowpane test.

Add cooked and cooled millet

- Dust the bench with some wholemeal flour, add the cooked and cooled millet and mix well.
- Rest for another 30 minutes.

Adjust flour or water (if necessary)

- If after the 30-minute rest period the dough still feels wet or too dry, add more flour or water. I find the best way to do this is to dip your hands in the water or flour and re-knead the dough until it feels right.

Shape   5 mins

- Divide the dough into three portions. Shape each dough portion into a ball and let it rest for about 20 minutes to relax the gluten.
- Stretch the dough to a rectangle of 20 x 25cm (8 x 10in).
- Roll tightly as though you were rolling a Swiss roll, close the seam well by pressing the edges together.
- Gently place onto baking paper.
- Mist the surface of the dough with water.

First and final rise   4–6 hours

- Let the dough rise until almost doubled—the time taken will vary.

Bake

- Preheat oven to 235°C (455°F) for at least 30 minutes. Prepare a water bath in a shallow oven tray and place in the oven.
- Bake for about 10 minutes, then reduce the oven to 210°C (410°F) for a further 20–25 minutes.
- Time for baking will vary.
- Remove the loaves the from the oven, immediately invert loaves onto a cooling rack, taking care not to burn yourself!
- If you are unsure whether the loaves have cooked through, turn the oven off and let them sit in the oven for a further 10 minutes.

Rest

- Let the bread cool on a rack before cutting.

Bread is suitable for freezing and will keep for a couple of months frozen.

burghul wheat sourdough

*Burghul (cracked wheat) or freekeh (cracked green wheat)
adds nuttiness and crunchy texture to an ordinary sourdough loaf.
It is worth the extra step to soak and cook the grains as this eliminates
phytates, allowing full absorption of vitamins and minerals in
wholegrains. This loaf marries well with hummus.*

burghul wheat sourdough

Ingredients

150g (5.3oz) rye starter (made with 1:1.5 flour to water ratio)

360g (12fl oz) water

300g (10.5oz) unbleached white spelt/wheat flour

300g (10.5oz) wholewheat spelt flour

225g soaked, cooked burghul or frekkeh

3 teaspoons (15g) sea salt

1350g (47.5oz) makes three small or 2 large free-form loaves

Method

Measure ingredients

- Using, preferably, a digital scale, weigh all ingredients including, water. Put all ingredients in a non-metallic bowl, starting with water and starter, flour and then salt last.

Mix ingredients 2–3 mins

- Using a spatula or wooden spoon, stir the ingredients together until they form a cohesive mass.

Rest 15–20 mins

- Rest the dough in the bowl for 15–20 minutes. This step allows the flour to absorb the water.

Kneading—air kneading 5 mins

- This dough is wet and you may find it easier to oil the work surface or bench and your hands.
- Using your fingertips, throw the dough into the air and then slap/throw it onto the bench.
- Repeat this action for about 5 minutes until the dough develops some elasticity.

Rest 20–30 mins

- As a general rule, 20 minutes rest is sufficient. However, if your dough is still sticky, do a longer rise—this step relaxes the gluten and giving the gluten strands a chance to re-align themselves.
- Your dough should feel soft, elastic and slightly sticky.
- Do a windowpane test.
- Dust your bench with some wholemeal flour, add the cooked and cooled burghul or frekkeh and mix well.

Adjust flour or water (if necessary)

- If after the rest period the dough still feels wet or too dry, add more flour or water. I find the best way to do this is to dip your hands in the water or flour and re-knead the dough until it feels right.

Shape   5 mins

- Divide into two or three portions. Shape each dough portion into a ball, let it rest for about 20 minutes to relax the gluten.
- Stretch the dough to a rectangle of 20x25cm (8x10 inches).
- Roll tightly as though you were rolling a Swiss roll, close the seam well by pressing the edges together.
- Gently place onto baking paper.
- Mist the surface of the dough with water.

First and final rise   4–6 hours

- Let dough rise until almost doubled—the time taken will vary.

Bake

- Preheat your oven to 235°C (455°F) for at least 30 minutes, prepare a water bath in an shallow oven tray and place it in the oven.
- Bake in a hot oven, which has been preheated at 235°C (455°F) for about 10 minutes, then reduce the oven to 210°C (410°F) for a further 20–25 minutes
- Time for baking will vary.
- Remove the loaves from the oven and immediately invert loaves onto a cooling rack, taking care not to burn yourself!
- If you are unsure whether the loaf has cooked through, turn the oven off and let it sit in the oven for a further 10 minutes.

Rest

- Let the bread cool before cutting.

Bread is suitable for freezing and will keep for a couple of months frozen.

half 'n' half wheat and spelt sourdough

The white spelt gives this bread great elasticity, but the wholewheat gives this bread the ultimate sweetness. This is one of my favourite breads and one of the most beautiful doughs to knead.

You can use either whole rye or whole spelt starter in this recipe. Rye starter will give you a more complex flavour while the spelt starter will give you a lighter loaf with a better rise.

half 'n' half wheat and spelt sourdough

Ingredients

150g (5oz) rye starter culture
(made with 1:1.5 flour to water ratio)

or

150g (5oz) whole spelt starter
(made with 1:1 flour to water ratio),
for a lighter bread

400g (14oz) organic unbleached
white spelt flour

400g (14oz) organic whole-wheat
flour, preferably coarsely milled.

500g (17fl oz) filtered water,
room temperature

3 teaspoons (15g) sea salt,
finely ground

1465g (52oz) 2 loaves of approx
700g (25oz) or one medium
sandwich loaf (450g/16oz baker's tin)

Method

Measure ingredients

- Using, preferably, a digital scale, weigh all ingredients, including the water. Put all ingredients in a non-metallic bowl, starting with water and starter, flour and the salt last.

Mix ingredients   2–3 mins

- Using a spatula or wooden spoon, stir the ingredients together until they form a cohesive mass.

Rest   15–20 mins

- Rest the dough in the bowl for 15–20 minutes. This step allows the flour to absorb the water.

Kneading—air kneading   5 mins

- This dough is wet and you may find it easier to oil the work surface or bench and your hands.
- Using your fingertips, throw the dough into the air and then slap/throw it onto the bench.
- Repeat this action for about 5 minutes until the dough develops some elasticity.

Rest   20–30 mins

- Rest the dough. As a general rule, 20 minutes rest is sufficient. However, if the dough is still sticky, do a longer rise—this step relaxes the gluten and giving the gluten strands a chance to re-align themselves.
- The dough should feel soft, elastic and slightly sticky.

Adjust flour or water (if necessary)

- If after the 30-minute rest period the dough still feels wet or too dry, add more water or flour. I find the best way to do this is to dip your hands in the water or flour and re-knead the dough until it feels right.

Final kneading (if necessary)   3–5 mins

- If the dough isn't elastic, soft and looks silky smooth, air knead further.
- Do a windowpane test.

First rise   4–6 hours

- Let the dough rises until almost doubled—the time taken will vary.

Shape   5 mins

- Shape the dough into a ball, let it rest for about 20 minutes to relax the gluten.
- Stretch the dough to a rectangle of 20 x 25cm (8 x 10in)
- Roll tightly as though you were rolling a Swiss roll, close the seam well by pressing the edges together.
- Gently lift the roll into the tin, then roll it around inside the tin to fit it evenly.
- Mist the surface of the dough with water, then sprinkle with seeds if you wish.

Final rise   2 hours

- Let the dough rise until almost doubled—the time taken will vary.

Bake

- Preheat oven to 235°C (455°F).
- Place the dough in the oven. Bake for about 15 minutes, then reduce the oven to 215°C (410°F) for a further 30–40 minutes until the bread is cooked through.
- Time taken for baking will vary.
- The loaf should be brown/golden brown all over and sound hollow when knocked on the bottom.
- Remove tin from oven, immediately invert loaf onto a cooling rack, taking care not to burn yourself.
- If you are unsure whether the loaf has cooked through, turn the oven off and let it sit in the oven for a further 10 minutes.

Rest

- Let the bread cool on a rack before cutting.

Bread is suitable for freezing and will keep for a couple of months frozen.

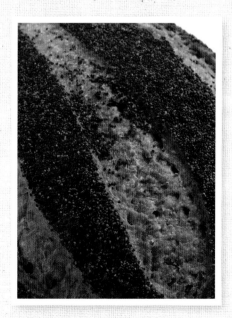

Wheat-free sourdough breads

spelt sourdough casalinga bread

This spelt sourdough bread is one of my daily breads because it tastes so good. It is so easy to make and the spelt gives the dough such elasticity that it is a pleasure to knead. The caramel-like flavour of spelt really shines through. You can use either rye or whole spelt starter. The spelt starter gives a better volume and a less acidic flavour. Rye starter adds complexity to the flavour.

Ingredients

200g (7oz) rye starter culture
(made with 1:1.5 flour to water ratio)

or

200g (7oz) whole spelt starter
(made with 1:1 flour to water ratio)

800g (27oz) organic unbleached
white spelt flour

500g (17fl oz) filtered water, room
temperature

3 teaspoons (15g) sea salt,
finely ground

1515g (53.5oz) makes 3 small or
2 medium loaves

Method

Measure ingredients

- Using, preferably, a digital scale, weigh all ingredients, including the water. Put all ingredients in a non-metallic bowl, starting with water and starter, flour and the salt last.

Mix ingredients   2–3 mins

- Using a spatula or wooden spoon, stir the ingredients together until they form a cohesive mass.

Rest   15–20 mins

- Rest the dough in the bowl for 15–20 minutes. This step is most important for wholegrain/wholemeal dough, allowing a greater absorption of water.

Kneading—air kneading   5 mins

- Using your fingertips, throw the dough into the air and then slap/throw it onto the bench. You may find it easier to oil the bench and your hands.
- After you have done this for about 5 minutes, the dough will have developed some elasticity.

Rest   20–30 mins

- Rest the dough. As a general rule, 20 minutes rest is sufficient. However, if the dough is still sticky, rest for longer. This step relaxes the gluten and giving the gluten strands a chance to re-align themselves.
- The dough should feel soft, elastic and slightly sticky.

Adjust flour or water (if necessary)

- If after the 30-minute rest period the dough still feels wet or too dry, add more water or flour. I find the best way to do this is to dip your hands in the water or flour and re-knead the dough until it feels right.

Final kneading (if necessary)   3–5 mins

- If the dough isn't elastic, soft and looks silky smooth, air knead further.
- Do a windowpane test.
- Gather the dough together and try to make a ball, let it rest in a covered non-metallic container or a bowl covered with a wet tea towel or cling wrap.

First rise   4–6 hours

- Let the dough rises until almost doubled—the time taken will vary.

Divide and shape   5 mins

- Divide the dough into two or three pieces. Shape the loaves as desired.
- Gently slip the dough onto baking paper.

Second/final rise   2 hours

- Rise again until almost doubled. This will take about 2 hours at a comfortable room temperature of 20–25°C (70–80°F), make sure the dough is covered or mist with water to prevent drying.

Bake

- Preheat oven to 235°C (455°F).
- Bake for about 10 minutes, then reduce the oven to 225°C (455°F) for a further 15–20 minutes for the small loaves, 30–35 minutes for the medium loaves.
- Time for baking will vary. The loaves should be brown/golden brown all over and sound hollow when knocked on the bottom.
- If you are unsure whether the loaf has cooked through, turn the oven off and let it sit in the oven for a further 10 minutes.
- Remove the loaves from the oven, taking care not to burn yourself!

Rest

- Let the bread cool on a rack before cutting.

Bread is suitable for freezing and will keep for a couple of months frozen.

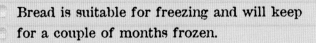

light rye spelt sourdough

Most commercial yeasted or sourdough rye breads have less than 15 per cent rye flour in them, including the darker rye loaves, which have been coloured with either caramel, coffee or roasted barley malt powder.

This bread has about 25 per cent rye of the total flour used, just enough rye to give a slight acidic tang, silky texture and a grey-blonde crumb colour. It is also fabulous as a sandwich bread.

Ingredients

300g (11oz) rye starter culture
(made with 1:1.5 flour to water ratio)

500g (18oz) organic unbleached
white spelt flour

250g (8.5fl oz) filtered water, room
temperature

3 teaspoons (15g) sea salt,
finely ground

1065g (38oz) makes two free-form
loaves or one small sandwich loaf
(340g baker's tin)

Method

Measure ingredients

- Using, preferably, a digital scale, weigh all ingredients, including the water. Put all ingredients in a non-metallic bowl, starting with water and starter, flour and then salt last.

Mix ingredients   2–3 mins

- Using a spatula or wooden spoon, stir the ingredients together until they form a cohesive mass.

Rest   15–20 mins

- Rest the dough in the bowl for 15–20 minutes. This step allows the flour to absorb the water.

Kneading—air kneading   5 mins

- This dough is wet and you may find it easier to oil the work surface or bench and your hands.
- Using your fingertips, throw the dough into the air and then slap/throw it onto the bench.
- Repeat this action for about 5 minutes until the dough develops some elasticity.

Rest   20–30 mins

- Rest the dough. As a general rule, 20 minutes rest is sufficient. However, if the dough is still sticky, rest for longer. This step relaxes the gluten and giving the gluten strands a chance to re-align themselves.

- The dough should feel soft, elastic and slightly sticky.
- Do a windowpane test.

First and final rise   4–6 hours
- Let the dough rises until almost doubled—the time taken will vary.

Shape   5 mins
- Divide the dough into two for free-form loaves. Shape each dough portion into a ball, let it rest for about 20 minutes to relax the gluten.
- For the free-form loaf, stretch the dough into a rectangle 20 x 25cm (8 x 10in).
- Roll tightly as though you were rolling a Swiss roll. Close the seam well by pressing the edges together.
- Gently lift the roll into the tin for sandwich bread then roll it around inside the tin to fit it evenly.
- For free-form loaves, place onto baking paper.
- Mist the surface of the dough with water, then sprinkle with grains/seeds if you wish.

Bake
- Preheat oven to 235°C (455°F).
- For free-form loaves, bake for about 10 minutes, then reduce the oven to 210°C (410°F) for a further 20–25 minutes.
- For the sandwich loaf, bake for about 10 minutes, then reduce the oven to 210°C (410°F) for a further 25–30 minutes.
- Time for baking will vary.
- Remove the tin from the oven, immediately invert loaf onto a cooling rack, taking care not to burn yourself!
- If you are unsure whether the loaf has cooked through, turn the oven off and let it sit in the oven for a further 10 minutes.

Rest
- Let the bread cool on a rack before cutting.

Bread is suitable for freezing and will keep for a couple of months frozen.

dark rye spelt sourdough

This rye sourdough is reminiscent of rye bread in northern Europe. Its flavour is tangy, complex and somewhat sweet, its colour is beautiful dark tan, with an even darker black/brown thick crust. It is dense, chewy and moist bread, having about 50 per cent rye in the total flour used. The dough will feel sticky and somewhat tacky, like elastic. Don't be alarmed.

Ingredients

500g (18oz) rye starter culture (made with 1:1.5 flour to water ratio)

100g whole rye flour

400g (14oz) organic whole spelt flour, preferably stone-ground

200g (6½fl oz) filtered water, room temperature

1–2 tablespoons liquid barley malt

3 teaspoons (15g) sea salt, finely ground

2–3 teaspoons carraway seeds added to the dough in the final kneading (optional)

―――――――――――――

1225g (43oz) makes two small free form loaves

Method

Measure ingredients

- Using, preferably, a digital scale, weigh all ingredients, including the water. Put all ingredients in a non-metallic bowl, starting with water and starter, flour and then salt last.

Mix ingredients   2–3 mins

- Using a spatula or wooden spoon, stir the ingredients together until they form a cohesive mass.

Rest   15–20 mins

- Rest the dough in the bowl for 15–20 minutes. This step allows the flour to absorb the water.

Kneading—air kneading   5 mins

Note: Although this very wet dough can be kneaded by hand, I recommend kneading with a bread-making machine or a rotary mixer.

- This dough is wet and you may find it easier to oil the work surface or bench and your hands.
- Using your fingertips, throw the dough into the air and then slap/throw it onto the bench.
- Repeat this action for about 5 minutes until the dough develops some elasticity.

Rest   20–30 mins

- Rest the dough. As a general rule, 20 minutes rest is sufficient. However, if the dough is still sticky, rest for longer. This step relaxes the gluten and giving the gluten strands a chance to re-align themselves.
- The dough should feel soft, elastic and slightly sticky.

Adjust flour or water (if necessary)

- If after the 30-minute rest period the dough still feels wet or too dry, add more water or flour. I find the best way to do this is to dip your hands in the water or flour and re-knead the dough until it feels right.

Final kneading (if necessary)   3–5 mins

- If the dough isn't elastic, soft and looks silky smooth, air knead further.
- Do a windowpane test.

First and final rise   4–6 hours

- Scoop all of the dough with a large dough scraper put it directly into a flour dusted or oiled bench
- Using wet hands and a large dough scraper, divide the dough in two, shape into a round or a baton.
- Let the dough rise until almost doubled—the time taken will vary.

Bake

- Preheat the oven to 235°C (455°F) for at least 30 minutes, prepare a water bath in an shallow oven tray and place it in the oven.
- Bake the loaves in a hot oven which for about 10 minutes, then reduce the oven to 210°C (410°F) for a further 30–35 minutes until the bread is cooked through and quite dark brown in colour.
- Remove the loaves from the oven, immediately invert loaves onto a cooling rack, taking care not to burn yourself!
- If you are unsure whether the loaf has cooked through, turn the oven off and let it sit in the oven for a further 10 minutes.

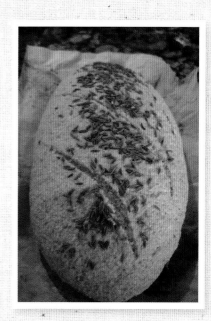

Rest

- Let the bread cool on a rack before cutting.

Bread is suitable for freezing and will keep for a couple of months frozen.

whole spelt, rye and barley sourdough bread with sunflower seeds

The three grains give this bread a complete balance of flavour and texture. Barley gives sweetness and nuttiness, spelt provides elasticity and volume, rye imparts a distinctive sour tang and a silkiness to the texture of this bread. The sunflower seeds add nuttiness and crunch.

whole spelt, rye and barley sourdough with sunflower seeds

Ingredients

300g (11oz) thin and active rye starter culture (1:15) flour to water ratio

400g (14oz) organic wholemeal spelt flour, preferably stone-ground

200g (7oz) organic whole barley flour

300g (10fl oz) filtered water, room temperature

3 teaspoons (15g) sea salt, finely ground

Add after kneading:
150g (5oz) sunflower seeds (toasted lightly)

1365g (48oz) makes one sandwich loaf or two small free-form loaf

Method

Measure ingredients

- Using, preferably, a digital scale, weigh all ingredients, including the water. Put all ingredients in a non-metallic bowl, starting with water and starter, flour and then salt last.

Mix ingredients   2–3 mins

- Using a spatula or wooden spoon, stir the ingredients together until they form a cohesive mass.

Rest   15–20 mins

- Rest the dough in the bowl for 15–20 minutes. This step allows the flour to absorb the water.

Kneading—air kneading   5 mins

- This dough is wet and you may find it easier to oil the work surface or bench and your hands.
- Using your fingertips, throw the dough into the air and then slap/throw it onto the bench.
- Repeat this action for about 5 minutes until the dough develops some elasticity.

Rest   20–30 mins

- Rest the dough. As a general rule, 20 minutes rest is sufficient. However, if the dough is still sticky, rest for longer. This step relaxes the gluten and giving the gluten strands a chance to re-align themselves.
- The dough should feel soft, elastic and slightly sticky.
- Do a windowpane test.

Add sunflower seeds

- Dust the bench with some wholemeal flour, add sunflower seeds and mix well.
- Rest for about 30 minutes. If after the 30-minute rest period the dough still feel wet or dry, add more water or flour. I find the best way

to do this is to dip your hands in the water or flour and re-knead the dough until it feels right.

Shape   5 mins

- Divide the dough into two for free-form loaves. Shape each dough portions into a ball, let it rest for about 20 minutes to relax the gluten.
- For the sandwich loaf, stretch the dough to a rectangle of 20 x 25cm (8 x10in). Roll tightly as though you were rolling a Swiss roll. Close the seam well by pressing the edges together.
- Gently lift the roll into the tin for sandwich bread then roll it around inside the tin to fit it evenly.
- For free-form loaves, place onto baking paper.
- Mist the surface of the dough with water, then sprinkle with grains/ seeds if you wish.

First and final rise   4–6 hours

- Let the dough rise until almost doubled—the time taken will vary.

Bake

- Preheat oven to 235°C (455°F).
- For sandwich loaves, bake for about 10 minutes, then reduce the oven to 210°C (410°F) for a further 25–30 minutes.
- For free-form loaves, bake for about 10 minutes, then reduce the oven to 210°C (410°F) for a further 20–25 minutes.
- Time for baking will vary. The loaves should be brown/golden brown all over and sound hollow when knocked on the bottom.
- Remove the tin from the oven, immediately invert loaf onto a cooling rack, taking care not to burn yourself!
- If you are unsure whether the loaf has cooked through, turn the oven off and let it sit in the oven for a further 10 minutes.

Rest

- Let the bread cool on a rack before cutting.

Bread is suitable for freezing and will keep for a couple of months frozen.

two-way barley spelt sourdough

This very special sourdough bread combines the sweetness of barley flour and the chewy crunch of cooked or sprouted barley. The spelt flour gives this bread a good volume, compensating for the low gluten in barley.

Ingredients

200g (7oz) whole-spelt starter
(made with 1:1 flour to water ratio)

480g (16fl oz) filtered water

250g (9oz) soaked and cooked
barley (cooled) or sprouted barley

150g (5oz) unbleached white
spelt flour

700g (25oz) wholemeal spelt flour

3 teaspoons (15g) sea salt

Extra wholemeal flour for dusting

1785g (63oz) makes three
free-form loaves

Method

Measure ingredients

- Using, preferably, a digital scale, weigh all ingredients, including the water. Put all ingredients in a non-metallic bowl, starting with water and starter, flour and then salt last.

Mix ingredients   2–3 mins

- Using a spatula or wooden spoon, stir the ingredients together until they form a cohesive mass.

Rest   15–20 mins

- Rest the dough in the bowl for 15–20 minutes. This step allows the flour to absorb the water.

Kneading—air kneading   5 mins

- This dough is wet and you may find it easier to oil the work surface or bench and your hands.
- Using your fingertips, throw the dough into the air and then slap/throw it onto the bench.
- Repeat this action for about 5 minutes until the dough develops some elasticity.

Rest   20–30 mins

- Rest the dough. As a general rule, 20 minutes rest is sufficient. However, if the dough is still sticky, rest for longer. This step relaxes the gluten and giving the gluten strands a chance to re-align themselves.
- The dough should feel soft, elastic and slightly sticky.
- Do a windowpane test.

Add the barley

- Dust the bench with some wholemeal flour, add the cooked and cooled barley and mix well.
- Rest for about 30 minutes. If after the 30-minute rest period the dough still feels wet or too dry, add more water or flour. I find the best way to do this is to dip your hands in the water or flour and re-knead the dough until it feels right.

First and final rise   4–6 hours

- Let the dough rise until almost doubled—the time taken will vary.

Shape   5 mins

- Divide into three portions. Shape each dough portion into a ball and let it rest for about 20 minutes to relax the gluten.
- Stretch the dough to a rectangle of 20 x 25cm (8 x 10in)
- Roll tightly as though you were rolling a Swiss roll, close the seam well by pressing the edges together.
- Gently place onto baking paper.
- Mist the surface of the dough with water

Bake

- Preheat oven to 235°C (455°F).
- Bake for about 10 minutes, then reduce the oven to 210°C (410°F) for a further 20–25 minutes.
- Time for baking will vary. The loaves should be brown/golden brown all over and sound hollow when knocked on the bottom.
- Immediately invert loaf onto a cooling rack, taking care not to burn yourself.
- If you are unsure whether the loaf has cooked through, turn the oven off and let it sit in the oven for a further 10 minutes.

Rest

- Let the bread cool on a rack before cutting.

Bread is suitable for freezing and will keep for a couple of months frozen.

light rye, barley and spelt sourdough

Both rye and barley contain very little gluten compared to wheat/spelt. To compensate for this, spelt gives this bread the gluten it needs to rise well. Whole rye and barley flour give it unique flavour. This is my daughter's favourite bread.

Ingredients

150g (5oz) unbleached white spelt starter (made with 1:1 flour to water ratio)

500g (18oz) organic unbleached white spelt flour

200g (7oz) organic whole-barley flour

100g (3.5oz) organic whole-rye flour

500g (17fl oz) filtered water, room temperature

1 tablespoon organic dark barley malt

3 teaspoons (15g) sea salt, finely ground

1465g (52oz) makes 2 loaves of approx 700g (25oz)

Method

Measure ingredients

- Using, preferably, a digital scale, weigh all ingredients, including the water. Put all ingredients in a non-metallic bowl, starting with water and starter, flour and then salt last.

Mix ingredients   2–3 mins

- Using a spatula or wooden spoon, stir the ingredients together until they form a cohesive mass.

Rest   15–20 mins

- Rest the dough in the bowl for 15–20 minutes. This step allows the flour to absorb the water.

Kneading—air kneading   5 mins

- This dough is wet and you may find it easier to oil the work surface or bench and your hands.
- Using your fingertips, throw the dough into the air and then slap/throw it onto the bench.
- Repeat this action for about 5 minutes until the dough develops some elasticity.

Rest   20–30 mins

- Rest the dough. As a general rule, 20 minutes rest is sufficient. However, if the dough is still sticky, rest for longer. This step relaxes the gluten and givies the gluten strands chance to re-align themselves.
- The dough should feel soft, elastic and slightly sticky.
- Do a windowpane test.

Divide and shape   5 mins

- Divide into three portions. Shape each dough portion into a ball, let it rest for about 20 minutes to relax the gluten.
- Stretch the dough to a rectangle of 20x25cm (8x10in)
- Roll tightly as though you were rolling a Swiss roll, close the seam well by pressing the edges together.
- Gently place onto baking paper.
- Mist the surface of the dough with water

First and final rise   4–6 hours

- Let the dough rise until almost doubled—the time taken will vary.

Bake

- Preheat oven to 235°C (455°F).
- Bake for about 10 minutes, then reduce the oven to 210°C (410°F) for a further 20–25 minutes.
- Time for baking will vary. The loaves should be brown/golden brown all over and sound hollow when knocked on the bottom.
- Immediately invert loaf onto a cooling rack, taking care not to burn yourself!
- If you are unsure whether the loaf has cooked through, turn the oven off and let it sit in the oven for a further 10 minutes.

Rest

- Let the bread cool on a rack before cutting.

Bread is suitable for freezing and will keep for a couple of months frozen.

crusty kamut and spelt sourdough

For those of you who love store-bought crusty Italian loaves but are intolerant of wheat, this is the bread for you. The two-step fermentation makes it even more digestible. This bread has a soft crumb with a thick crust. The flavour is complex with a hint of caramel sweetness, characteristic of spelt, with only a very mild sour tang. Kamut flour gives this bread a chewier and thicker crust and a golden glow.

crusty kamut and spelt sourdough

Ingredients

200g (7oz) whole spelt starter culture

500g (18oz) organic unbleached white spelt flour

300g (11oz) organic fine kamut flour

550g (19fl oz) filtered water, room temperature

3 teaspoons (15g) sea salt, finely ground

1565g (55oz) makes two medium-size loaves

Method

Measure ingredients

• Using, preferably, a digital scale, weigh all ingredients, including the water. Put all ingredients in a non-metallic bowl, starting with water and starter, flour and then salt last.

Mix ingredients   2–3 mins

• Using a spatula or wooden spoon, stir the ingredients together until they form a cohesive mass.

Rest   30 mins

• Rest the dough in the bowl for 30 minutes. This step allows the semolina flour to absorb the water.

Kneading—air kneading   5 mins

• This dough is wet and you may find it easier to oil the work surface or bench and your hands.
• Using your fingertips, throw the dough into the air and then slap/throw it onto the bench.
• Repeat this action for about 5 minutes until the dough develops some elasticity.

Rest   20–30 mins

• Rest the dough for another 30 minutes. This relaxes the gluten and gives the gluten strands a chance to re-align themselves.
• Your dough should feel soft, elastic and slightly sticky.

Adjust flour or water (if necessary)

• If, after the 30-minute rest period, your dough still feels wet or too dry, add a small amount of water or flour. I find the best way to do this is to dip your hands in the water or flour and re-knead the dough until it feels right.

Final kneading (if necessary)   3–5 mins

• If the dough isn't elastic, soft and looking silky smooth, air knead further.
• Do a windowpane test.

Shape   5 mins

- Dust your bench generously with kamut flour, invert the dough onto the bench and dust the dough with more flour.
- Using floured hands, shape the dough into a round loaf or tow separate loaves, and scoop the dough onto baking paper.
- Dust the loaf generously with more kamut flour.

Final rise   4 hrs

- Let the dough rise until doubled—the time taken will vary—don't be alarmed though, the dough will look flat as it increases in size.
- You may see a crack on the surface of the dough. This is a sign that it is almost ready.
- Do an indentation test.

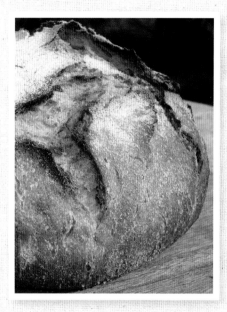

Bake

- Preheat oven to 235°C (455°F).
- Place the granite tile in the bottom of the oven to heat up. This may take up to 30 minutes.
- Place the dough on the granite in the bottom of the oven with a water bath on the top rack. Cook for 12–15 minutes until the bottom crust is brown.
- Reduce the oven to 225°C (437°F), move the loaf to a higher rack and bake for a further 20–25 minutes until cooked through.
- The loaf should be brown/golden brown all over and sound hollow when knocked on the bottom.
- If you are unsure whether the loaf has cooked through, turn the oven off and let it sit in the oven for a further 10 minutes.
- Remove the loaf from the oven, taking care not to burn yourself!

Rest

- Let the bread cool on a rack before cutting.

Bread is suitable for freezing and will keep for a couple of months frozen.

Savoury sourdough breads

haloumi and mint sourdough

I do this bread in my beginners class and from day one, this loaf has been the favourite of all my students. This is an authentic Cypriot bread, the flavour of mint marries well with the saltiness of haloumi cheese. Haloumi cheese works well baked in bread because it will slightly melt but will keep its shape.

Using the same dough, you can substitute haloumi and mint with salted olives and roasted onions. This is another bread that I also make in the beginners' class, using the same dough.

Ingredients

200g (7oz) rye starter culture (made with 1:1.5 flour to water ratio)

800g organic unbleached ATTA flour or light wholemeal

or

400g (14oz) organic wholemeal wheat/spelt, and

400g (14oz) organic unbleached white wheat/spelt

500ml (17fl oz) filtered water, room temperature

3 teaspoons (15g) sea salt, finely ground

1350g makes 2 loaves of bread

250–300g (11oz) haloumi (or more if you prefer), chopped into small cubes

1 tablespoon dried Greek mint or a mixture of 2 teaspoons oregano and 1 teaspoon mint

Method

Measure ingredients

• Using, preferably, a digital scale, weigh all ingredients, including the water. Put all ingredients in a non-metallic bowl, starting with water and starter, flour and the salt last.

Mix ingredients   2–3 mins

• Using a spatula or wooden spoon, stir the ingredients together until they form a cohesive mass.

Rest   15–20 mins

• Rest the dough in the bowl for 15–20 minutes. This step is most important for wholegrain/wholemeal dough, allowing a greater absorption of water.

Kneading—air kneading   5 mins

• Using your fingertips, throw the dough into the air and then slap/throw it onto the bench. You may find it easier to oil the bench and your hands.
• After you have done this for about 5 minutes, the dough will have developed some elasticity.

Rest   20–30 mins

• Rest the dough. As a general rule, 20 minutes rest is sufficient. However, if the dough is still sticky, rest for longer. This step relaxes the gluten and giving the gluten strands a chance to re-align themselves.
• The dough should feel soft, elastic and slightly sticky.

Final kneading (if necessary)   3–5 mins

- If the dough isn't elastic, soft and looks silky smooth, air knead further.
- Do a windowpane test.
- Gather the dough together and try to make a ball, let it rest in a non-metallic container or a bowl covered with a wet tea towel or cling wrap.

First rise   4–6 hours

- Let the dough rise until almost doubled—the time taken will vary.

Divide and shape   5 mins

- Divide the dough into two or three x 600g (22oz) pieces. Shape the loaves as desired.
- Stretch each piece into a rectangular roll about 22 x 25cm (9 x 10in). Arrange the chopped haloumi and sprinkle the dried herbs on top.
- Like folding a Swiss roll, fold the haloumi and herbs into the dough, roll tightly to avoid air pockets and shape into a long roll. Make sure that the seams are closed well by pressing the edges together.

Second/final rise

- Rise again until almost doubled, about 2 hours at a comfortable room temperature around 20–25°C (70–80°F).

Bake

- Preheat oven to 235°C (455°F).
- Bake for 10–15 minutes, then reduce the oven to 225°C (437°F) for a further 30–35 minutes until cooked through.
- Time for baking will vary. The loaves should be brown/golden brown all over and sound hollow when knocked on the bottom.
- If you are unsure whether the loaves have cooked through, turn the oven off, and let them sit in the oven for a further 10 minutes.
- Remove loaves from oven, taking care not to burn yourself!

Rest

- Let the bread cool on a rack before cutting.

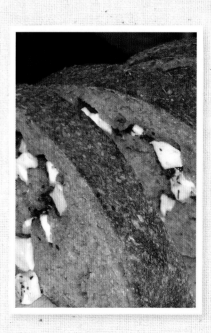

sweet-potato and cheddar sourdough loaf

This is one of those breads that will delight everyone. The sweetness of sweet potato or pumpkin will shine through the bread. It has a beautiful bright yellow/orange colour with streaks of melted cheddar cheese. If you like, you can substitute the cheddar with gruyère or fontina cheese. Eat warm with melted butter or more matured cheddar cheese.

Ingredients

150g (5oz) unbleached white wheat or spelt starter

150g (5oz) organic unbleached white spelt or wheat flour

650g (23oz) organic atta flour

200g (7oz) sweet potato or Japanese pumpkin, roasted at 180°C (360°F) for 20–25 minutes or until soft

400g (14fl oz) filtered water, room temperature

3 teaspoons (15g) sea salt, finely ground

1 tablespoon organic barley or brown rice malt

200g (7oz) matured cheddar cheese, roughly grated.

1800g (63.5oz) makes 3 small loaves

Method

Measure ingredients

- Using, preferably, a digital scale, weigh all ingredients, including the water. Put all ingredients in a non-metallic bowl, starting with water and starter, flour, mashed sweet potato or pumpkin and then salt last.

Mix ingredients   2–3 mins

- Using a spatula or wooden spoon, stir the ingredients together until they form a cohesive mass.

Rest   15–20 mins

- Rest the dough in the bowl for 15–20 minutes. This step is most important for wholegrain/wholemeal dough, allowing a greater absorption of water.

Kneading—air kneading   5 mins

- Using your fingertips, throw the dough into the air and then slap/throw it onto the bench. You may find it easier to oil the bench and your hands.
- After you have done this for about 5 minutes, the dough will have developed some elasticity.

Rest   20–30mins

- Rest the dough. As a general rule, 20 minutes rest is sufficient. However, if the dough is still sticky, rest for longer. This step relaxes the gluten and giving the gluten strands a chance to re-align themselves.
- The dough should feel soft, elastic and slightly sticky.

Adjust flour or water (if necessary)

- If after the 30-minute rest period the dough still feels wet or too dry, add more water or flour. I find the best way to do this is to dip your hands in the water or flour and re-knead the dough until it feels right.

Final kneading (if necessary)   3–5 mins

- If the dough isn't elastic, soft and looks silky smooth, air knead further.
- Do a windowpane test.

- Gather the dough together and try to make a ball, let it rest in a covered non-metallic container or a bowl covered with a wet tea towel or cling wrap.

First rise   4–6 hours
- Let the dough rise until almost doubled—the time taken will vary.

Divide and shape   5 mins
- Divide the dough into two or three x 600g (22oz) pieces. Shape the loaves as desired.
- Stretch each piece into a rectangular roll about 22 x 25cm (9 x 10in). Arrange the grated cheese on top.
- Like folding a Swiss roll, fold the cheese into the dough, roll tightly to avoid air pockets and shape into a long roll. Make sure that the seams are closed well by pressing the edges together.

Second/final rise
- Rise again until almost doubled, about 2 hours at a comfortable room temperature of around 20–25°C (70–80°F). Make sure the dough is covered or mist with water to prevent drying.

Bake
- Preheat oven to 235°C (455°F).
- Bake for 10–12 minutes, then reduce the oven to 225°C (437°F) for a further 25–30 minutes until cooked through.
- Time for baking will vary.
- The loaves should be brown/golden brown all over and sound hollow when knocked on the bottom.
- If you are unsure whether the loaves have cooked through, turn the oven off and let them sit in the oven for a further 10 minutes.
- Remove the loaves from the oven, taking care not to burn yourself!

Rest
- Let the bread cool on a rack before cutting.

potato, olive and sage sourdough

Potato adds softness to any bread, whether it is yeasted or sourdough. It also gives the bread a very nice flavour. Olives and sage marry well with the potato flavour. This is a more-ish bread, eaten warm with lashings of butter.

Ingredients

200g (7oz) white wheat/spelt starter

300g (11oz) cooked potato, mashed finely

600g (22oz) organic whole-wheat flour

200g (7oz) organic unbleached white flour (premium bakers flour)

400g (14fl oz) filtered water, room temperature

2–3 tablespoons extra virgin olive oil, optional

3 teaspoons (15g) sea salt, finely ground

Add after kneading:

150–200g (5–7oz) kalamata olives, pitted

2 tablespoons fresh sage, chopped roughly

1 tablespoon fresh sage, whole

1678g (59oz) makes 2 or 3 loaves

Method

Measure ingredients

- Using, preferably, a digital scale, weigh all ingredients, including the mashed potato. Put all ingredients in a non-metallic bowl, starting with water and starter, flour, mashed potato and then salt last.

Mix ingredients   2–3 mins

- Using a spatula or wooden spoon, stir the ingredients together until they form a cohesive mass.

Rest   15–20 mins

- Rest the dough in the bowl for 15–20 minutes. This step is most important for wholegrain/wholemeal dough, allowing a greater absorption of water.

Kneading—air kneading   5 mins

- Using your fingertips, throw the dough into the air and then slap/throw it onto the bench. You may find it easier to oil the bench and your hands.
- After you have done this for about 5 minutes, the dough will have developed some elasticity.

Rest   20–30 mins

- Rest the dough. As a general rule, 20 minutes rest is sufficient. However, if the dough is still sticky, rest for longer. This step relaxes the gluten and giving the gluten strands a chance to re-align themselves.
- The dough should feel soft, elastic and slightly sticky.

Adjust flour or water (if necessary)

- If after the 30-minute rest period the dough still feel wet or too dry, add more water or flour. I find the best way to do this is to dip your hands in the water or flour and re-knead the dough until it feels right.

- Add the pitted olives and sage.

Final kneading (if necessary)   3–5 mins

- If the dough isn't elastic, soft and looks silky smooth, air knead further.
- Do a windowpane test.
- Gather the dough together and try to make a ball, let it rest in a covered non-metallic container or a bowl covered with a wet tea towel or cling wrap.

First rise   4–6 hours

- Let the dough rise until almost doubled—the time taken will vary.

Divide and shape   5 mins

- Divide the dough into two or three x 600g (22oz) portions. Shape the loaves as desired.
- Stretch each piece into a rectangular roll about 22 x 25cm (9 x 10in). Arrange olives and sage on the dough,
- Roll the dough tightly to avoid air pockets, like folding a Swiss roll, and shape into a long roll. Close the seam by pressing the edges firmly together.

Second/final rise

- Rise again until almost doubled, about 2 hours at a comfortable room temperature of around 20–25°C (70–80°F). Make sure the dough is covered or mist with water to prevent drying.

Bake

- Preheat oven to 235°C (455°F).
- Bake for 10–12 minutes, then reduce the oven to 225°C (437°F) for a further 25–30 minutes until cooked through.
- Time for baking will vary. The loaves should be brown/golden brown all over and sound hollow when knocked on the bottom.
- If you are unsure whether the loaves have cooked through, turn the oven off, and let the loaves sit in the oven for a further 10 minutes.
- Remove loaves from oven, taking care not to burn yourself!

Rest

- Let the bread cool on a rack before cutting.

roasted vegetable sourdough loaf

This loaf was originally created from left-over roasted vegetables from my beginners' class. I always roast capsicum, pumpkin or sweet potato, onions (sometimes aubergine) for my class to use as toppings for pizza. I seem to always have leftovers, so this is the loaf I create with those leftovers. It is a beautiful loaf, almost a meal in itself.

Ingredients

200g (7oz) white starter culture, (ripe and at room temperature)

500g (17oz) organic unbleached white premium bakers flour

300g (11oz) organic fine semolina

500g (17fl oz) filtered water, room temperature

2 teaspoons (10g) sea salt, finely ground

Add after kneading:
1/2 cup each of roasted capsicum, pumpkin/sweet potato

1 roasted onion, chopped finely

70g (2¹/₂oz) pitted kalamata olives in brine

1550g (54¹/₂oz) 1 large or 2 medium size loaves

Method

Measure ingredients
- Using, preferably, a digital scale, weigh all ingredients, including the water. Put all ingredients in a non-metallic bowl, starting with water and starter, flour and then salt last.

Mix ingredients   2–3 mins
- Using a spatula or wooden spoon, stir the ingredients together until they form a cohesive mass.

Rest   15–20 mins
- Rest the dough in the bowl for 15–20 minutes. This step is most important for wholegrain/wholemeal dough, allowing a greater absorption of water.

Kneading—air kneading   5 mins
- Using your fingertips, throw the dough into the air and then slap/throw it onto the bench. You may find it easier to oil the bench and your hands.
- After you have done this for about 5 minutes, the dough will have developed some elasticity.

Rest   20–30 mins
- Rest the dough. As a general rule, 20 minutes rest is sufficient. However, if the dough is still sticky, rest for longer. This step relaxes the gluten and giving the gluten strands a chance to re-align themselves.
- The dough should feel soft, elastic and slightly sticky.

Adjust flour or water (if necessary)

- If after the 30-minute rest period the dough still feels wet or too dry, add more water or flour. I find the best way to do this is to dip your hands in the water or flour and re-knead the dough until it feels right.

Final kneading (if necessary)　　3–5 mins

- If the dough isn't elastic, soft and looks silky smooth, air knead further.
- Do a windowpane test.
- Gather the dough together and try to make a ball, let it rest in a covered non-metallic container or a bowl covered with a wet tea towel or cling wrap.

Divide and shape　　5 mins

- Divide the dough into two or three 600g (22oz) pieces. Shape the loaves as desired.
- Stretch each piece into a rectangular roll about 22 x 25cm (9 x 10in). Arrange the chopped roasted vegetables and olives on top of the dough.
- Like folding a Swiss roll, fold roasted vegetables and olives into the dough, roll tightly to avoid air pockets and shape into a long roll. Make sure that the seams are closed.

First/final rise

- Rise until almost doubled, about 4 hours at a comfortable room temperature of around 20–25°C (70–80°F). Make sure the dough is covered or mist with water to prevent drying.

Bake

- Preheat oven to 235°C (455°F).
- Bake for 10–15 minutes, then reduce the oven to 225°C (437°F) for a further 30–35 minutes until cooked through.
- Time for baking will vary. The loaves should be brown/golden brown all over and sound hollow when knocked on the bottom.
- If you are unsure whether the loaves have cooked through, turn the oven off, and let the loaves sit in the oven for a further 10 minutes.
- Remove loaves from oven, taking care not to burn yourself!

Rest

- Let the bread cool on a rack before cutting.

beetroot and feta sourdough loaf

This is a very dramatic loaf of bread, it is pinkish red in colour with small chunks of white feta. The beetroot lends an earthy and sweet flavour, which marries well with the salty feta cheese.

Ingredients

150g (5oz) rye starter culture

or

150g (5oz) unbleached white spelt starter (ripe and at room temperature), for a lighter bread

200g (7oz) raw beetroot, grated into fine strands

400g (14oz) organic atta flour

150ml (5fl oz) filtered water, room temperature

3 teaspoons (15g) sea salt, finely ground

150–200g (5–7oz) feta cheese, drained

1115g (39oz) makes 2 loaves

Method

Measure ingredients

- Using, preferably, a digital scale, weigh all ingredients, including the water. Put all ingredients in a non-metallic bowl, starting with water and starter, flour, beetroot and then salt last.

Mix ingredients   2–3 mins

- Using a spatula or wooden spoon, stir the ingredients together until they form a cohesive mass.

Rest   15–20 mins

- Rest the dough in the bowl for 15–20 minutes. This step is most important for wholegrain/wholemeal dough, allowing a greater absorption of water.

Kneading—air kneading   5 mins

- Using your fingertips, throw the dough into the air and then slap/throw it onto the bench. You may find it easier to oil the bench and your hands.
- After you have done this for about 5 minutes, the dough will have developed some elasticity.

Rest   20–30 mins

- Rest the dough. As a general rule, 20 minutes rest is sufficient. However, if the dough is still sticky, rest for longer. This step relaxes the gluten and gives the gluten strands a chance to re-align themselves.
- The dough should feel soft, elastic and slightly sticky.

Adjust flour or water (if necessary)

- If after the 30-minute rest period the dough still feel wet or too dry, add more water or flour. I find the best way to do this is to dip your hands in the water or flour and re-knead the dough until it feels right.

Final kneading (if necessary)   3–5 mins

- If the dough isn't elastic, soft and looks silky smooth, air knead further.
- Do a windowpane test.
- Gather the dough together and try to make a ball. Let it rest in a covered non-metallic container or a bowl covered with a wet tea towel or cling wrap.

First rise   4–6 hours

- Let the dough rise until almost doubled—the time taken will vary.

Divide and shape   5 mins

- Divide the dough into two or three 600g (22oz) pieces. Shape the loaves as desired.
- Stretch each piece into a rectangular roll about 22 x 25cm (9 x 10in). Arrange grated cheese on top. Like folding a Swiss roll, fold the cheese into the dough, roll tightly to avoid air pockets and shape into a long roll. Make sure that the seams are closed well by pressing together.

Second/final rise

- Rise again until almost doubled, about 2 hours at a comfortable room temperature of around 20–25°C (70–80°F). Make sure the dough is covered or mist with water to prevent drying.

Bake

- Preheat oven to 235°C (455°F).
- Bake for 10–12 minutes, then reduce the oven to 225°C (437°F) for a further 25–30 minutes until cooked through.
- Time for baking will vary. The loaves should be brown/golden brown all over and sound hollow when knocked on the bottom.
- If you are unsure whether the loaves have cooked through, turn the oven off, and let the loaves sit in the oven for a further 10 minutes.
- Remove loaves from oven, taking care not to burn yourself!

Rest

- Let the bread cool on a rack before cutting.

walnut spelt sourdough loaf

This is the very best walnut bread I have ever tasted. By incorporating walnut paste made from crushed walnut, the walnut flavour is infused into the loaf without being overpowering. It is the perfect bread for any cheese platter, especially a triple cream brie. For something different but equally spectacular in flavour, try substituting hazelnuts and hazelnut oil for the walnuts and walnut oil.

walnut spelt sourdough loaf

Ingredients

200g (7oz) rye starter culture

or

200g (7oz) unbleached white
spelt starter
(ripe and at room temperature),
for a lighter bread

500g (17oz) organic wholemeal
spelt flour

500g (17oz) organic unbleached
white spelt flour

500g (17fl oz) filtered water, room
temperature

3 teaspoons (15g) sea salt,
finely ground

2 tablespoons walnut oil (optional)

65g (2oz) organic walnuts, lightly
roasted and crushed to a paste

175g (6oz) organic walnuts, lightly
roasted and cooled

Method

Measure ingredients

- Using, preferably, a digital scale, weigh all ingredients, including the water. Put all ingredients in a non-metallic bowl, starting with water and starter, flour and then salt last.

Mix ingredients   2–3 mins

- Using a spatula or wooden spoon, stir the ingredients together until they form a cohesive mass.

Rest   30 mins

- Rest the dough in the bowl for 30 minutes. This step allows the semolina flour to absorb the water.

Kneading—air kneading   5 mins

- Using your fingertips, throw the dough into the air and then slap/ throw it onto the bench.
- After you have done this for about 5 minutes, the dough will have developed some elasticity.

Rest   20–30 mins

- Rest the dough for another 30 minutes. This step relaxes the gluten and gives the gluten strands a chance to re-align themselves.
- The dough should feel soft, elastic and slightly sticky.

Adjust flour or water (if necessary)

- If after the 30-minute rest period the dough still feels wet or too dry, add more water or flour. I find the best way to do this is to dip your hands in the water or flour and re-knead the dough until it feels right.

Final kneading (if necessary)   3–5 mins

- If the dough isn't elastic, soft and looks silky smooth, air knead further.
- Do a windowpane test.

Adding walnut   3–5 mins

- Add crushed walnut and walnut paste. Knead well to mix evenly throughout the dough.

Shape

- Divide the dough into two or three even pieces.
- Using floured hands, shape the dough into a round or oval loaf, scoop the loaves onto individual baking paper.

Final rise

- Let the dough rise until doubled in size.
- Do an indentation test.

Bake

- Preheat oven to 235°C (455°F).
- Bake on the granite at the bottom of the oven with a water bath on the top rack, for about 10–12 minutes until the bottom crust is brown.
- Reduce the oven to 225°C (437°F), move the loaf to a higher rack, bake for a further 20 minutes or more until cooked through.
- Time for baking will vary. The loaves should be brown/golden brown all over and sound hollow when knocked on the bottom.
- If you are unsure whether the loaves have cooked through, turn the oven off, and let the loaves sit in the oven for a further 10 minutes.
- Remove the loaves from the oven, taking care not to burn yourself!

Rest

- Let the bread cool on a rack before cutting.

Bread is suitable for freezing and will keep for a couple of months frozen.

feta and chilli sourdough loaf

This is a spicy and mildly chilli hot bread that marries well with a smooth, creamy and mildly flavoured soup like leek and potato soup. It will instantly warm a cold winter night.

feta and chilli sourdough loaf

Ingredients

200g (7oz) rye starter culture (made with 1:1.5 flour to water ratio)

800g organic unbleached atta flour or light wholemeal

or

400g (14oz) organic wholemeal wheat/spelt

400g (14oz) organic unbleached white wheat/spelt

500–550ml (17–19fl oz) filtered water at room temperature

3 teaspoons (15g) sea salt, finely ground

250–300g (11oz) feta (or more if you prefer), chopped into small cubes

1/2–1 teaspoon dry roasted chilli, crushed roughly

1/2 teaspoon sweet paprika powder

1/2–1 teaspoon cracked black pepper

1350–1400g makes 2 loaves of bread

Method

Measure ingredients
- Use, preferably, a digital scale, to weigh all ingredients, including water, put all ingredients in a non-metallic bowl, starting with water and starter, flour and then salt last.

Mix ingredients   2–3 mins
- Using a spatula or wooden spoon, stir the ingredients together until they form a cohesive mass.

Rest   15–20 mins
- Rest the dough in the bowl for 15–20 minutes. This step is most important for wholegrain/wholemeal dough, allowing a greater absorption of water.

Kneading—air kneading   5 mins
- Using your fingertips, throw your dough into the air and then slap/throw it onto your bench.
- After you have done this for about 5 minutes, the dough will have developed some elasticity. You may find it easier to oil your bench and your hands.

Rest   20–30 mins
- As a general rule, 20 minutes rest is sufficient. However, if your dough is still sticky, do a longer rise. This step relaxes the gluten and giving the gluten strands a chance to re-align themselves.
- Your dough should feel soft, elastic and slightly sticky.

Adjust flour or water (if necessary)
- If after the 30-minute rest period the dough still feels wet or too dry, add more water or flour. I find the best way to do this is to dip your hands in the water or flour and re-knead the dough until it feels right.

Final kneading (if necessary)   3–5 mins
- If the dough isn't elastic, soft and looks silky smooth, air knead further.

- Do a windowpane test.
- Gather your dough together and try to make a ball, let it rest in a covered non-metallic container or a bowl covered with a wet tea towel or cling wrap.

First rise   4–6 hours
- Let your dough rise until almost doubled—the time taken will vary.

Divide and shape   5 mins
- Divide the dough into two or three 600g (22oz) pieces. Shape the loaves as desired.
- Stretch each piece into a rectangular roll about 22 x 25cm (9 x 10in). Arrange the feta and sprinkle the chilli, paprika and black pepper on top.
- Like folding a Swiss roll, fold the feta and spices into the dough, roll tightly to avoid air pockets and shape into a long roll. Make sure that the seams are closed.

Second/final rise
- Rise again until almost doubled, about 2 hours at a comfortable room temperature of around 20–25°C (70–80°F). Make sure the dough is covered or mist with water to prevent drying.

Bake
- Bake in a hot oven which has been preheated at 235°C (455°F) for about 10–15 minutes, then reduce the oven to 225°C (437°F) for a further 30–35 minutes until cooked through.
- Time for baking will vary. The loaves should be brown/golden brown all over and sounds hollow when knocked on the bottom.
- If you are unsure whether the loaves have cooked through, turn the oven off, and let them sit in the oven for a further 10 minutes.
- Remove loaves from oven, taking care not to burn yourself!

Rest
- Let the bread cool on a rack before cutting.

Sweet sourdough breads

fig and walnut sourdough

This is a true classic combination of dried fruits and nuts, a breakfast favourite. The walnuts increase the protein content of the already nutritious sourdough, while the dried figs add sweetness and fibre, making this loaf a substantial, complete and delicious breakfast. I make this bread in my beginners' class and it has become a favourite of many of my students. Substitute figs with dates for a delicious variation.

fig and walnut sourdough

Ingredients

200g (7oz) rye starter culture
(made with1:1.5 flour to water ratio)

400g (14oz) organic unbleached
white wheat/spelt

400g (14oz) organic wholemeal
wheat/spelt

500g (17fl oz) filtered water
or apple juice, room temperature

3 teaspoons (15g) sea salt,
finely ground

Extra ingredients to add after the first rise:

300g (11oz) dried figs,
preferably organic

150g (5oz) walnuts, organic,
chopped roughly

Optional additions:

200g (7oz) sultanas, organic

2–3 tablespoons fennel seeds

1350–1400g (47½–49oz) makes
2–3 loaves

Method

Measure ingredients

- Using, preferably, a digital scale, weigh all ingredients, including the water. Put all ingredients in a non-metallic bowl, starting with water and starter, flour and the salt last.

Mix ingredients   2–3 mins

- Using a spatula or wooden spoon, stir the ingredients together until they form a cohesive mass.

Rest   15–20 mins

- Rest the dough in the bowl for 15–20 minutes. This step is most important for wholegrain/wholemeal dough, allowing a greater absorption of water.

Kneading—air kneading   5 mins

- Using your fingertips, throw the dough into the air and then slap/throw it onto the bench. You may find it easier to oil the bench and your hands.
- After you have done this for about 5 minutes, the dough will have developed some elasticity.

Rest   20–30 mins

- Rest the dough. As a general rule, 20 minutes rest is sufficient. However, if the dough is still sticky, rest for longer. This step relaxes the gluten and giving the gluten strands a chance to re-align themselves.
- The dough should feel soft, elastic and slightly sticky.

Adjust flour or water (if necessary)

- If after the 30-minute rest period the dough still feel wet or too dry, add more water or flour. I find the best way to do this is to dip your hands in the water or flour and re-knead the dough until it feels right.

Final kneading (if necessary)

- If the dough isn't elastic, soft and looks silky smooth, air knead further.

- Do a windowpane test.
- Gather the dough together and try to make a ball, let it rest in a covered non-metallic container or a bowl covered with a wet tea towel or cling wrap.

First rise   4–6 hours
- Let the dough rise until almost doubled—the time taken will vary.

Divide and shape   5 mins
- Divide the dough into two or three 600g (22oz) pieces. Shape the loaves as desired.
- Stretch each piece into a rectangular roll about 22 x 25cm (9x 10in). Arrange the dried fruits and nuts on top. Like folding a Swiss roll, fold the dried fruits and nuts into the dough. Roll tightly to avoid air pockets and shape into a long roll. Make sure that the seams are closed and avoid exposing the dried fruits and nuts.

Second/Final rise   2 hours
- Rise again until almost doubled, about 2 hours at a comfortable room temperature of around 20–25°C (70–80°F). Make sure the dough is covered or mist with water to prevent drying.

Bake
- Preheat oven to 235°C (455°F).
- Bake for about 10 minutes, then reduce to 210°C (410°F) for a further 20–25 minutes for the 600g (22oz) loaves.
- Time for baking will vary. The loaves should be brown/golden brown all over and sound hollow when knocked on the bottom.
- If you are unsure whether the loaves have cooked through, turn the oven off, and let the loaves sit in the oven for a further 10 minutes.
- Remove loaves from oven, taking care not to burn yourself!

Rest
- Let the bread cool on a rack before cutting.

Bread is suitable for freezing and will keep for a couple of months frozen.

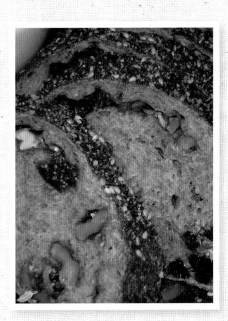

bitter chocolate, cranberry and pistachio spelt sourdough

This is my signature bread—somehow people seem to remember me from tasting this bread. Everyone who has tasted it cannot believe how delicious this sourdough is, even though there is not a hint of sweetness here. It is the bread for blue cheese or double/triple brie. Its slightly bitter and sour taste complements and cuts through the richness of the creamy cheese.

bitter chocolate, cranberry and pistachio spelt sourdough

Ingredients

150g (5oz) rye sourdough starter (made with 1:1.5 flour to water ratio)

750g (26½oz) organic unbleached white spelt flour

70g (2½oz) organic cocoa powder or best-quality cocoa powder (Vahlrona)

60g (2oz) organic barley malt

500g (17fl oz) filtered water

Added and mixed after first rise:
350g (12oz) organic dried cranberries

100g (3½oz) roasted nuts of your choice (eg. pistachio, pecan, hazelnut, almond). Soak overnight then roast at 70°C (158°F) for 7–10 hours or dry roast on the pan for a few minutes until fragrant.

150g (5oz) of dark chocolate (60–70 per cent cocoa), chopped roughly

Method

Measure ingredients

- Using, preferably, a digital scale, weigh all ingredients, including the water. Put all ingredients in a non-metallic bowl, starting with water and starter, flour and the salt last.

Mix ingredients   2–3 mins

- Using a spatula or wooden spoon, stir the ingredients together until they form a cohesive mass.

Rest   15–20 mins

- Rest the dough in the bowl for 15–20 minutes. This step is most important for wholegrain/wholemeal dough, allowing a greater absorption of water.

Kneading—air kneading   5 mins

- Using your fingertips, throw the dough into the air and then slap/throw it onto the bench. You may find it easier to oil the bench and your hands.
- After you have done this for about 5 minutes, the dough will have developed some elasticity.

Rest   20–30 mins

- Rest the dough. As a general rule, 20 minutes rest is sufficient. However, if the dough is still sticky, rest for longer. This step relaxes the gluten and giving the gluten strands a chance to re-align themselves.
- The dough should feel soft, elastic and slightly sticky.

Adjust flour or water (if necessary)

- If after the 30-minute rest period the dough still feels wet or too dry, add more water or flour. I find the best way to do this is to dip your hands in the water or flour and re-knead the dough until it feels right.

Final kneading (if necessary)   3–5 mins

- If the dough isn't elastic, soft and looks silky smooth, air knead further.

- Do a windowpane test.
- Gather the dough together and try to make a ball, let it rest in a covered non-metallic container or a bowl covered with a wet tea towel or cling wrap.

First rise   4–6 hours

- Let the dough rise until almost doubled—the time taken will vary.

Divide and shape   5 mins

- Add the cranberry, nuts and bitter chocolate pieces into the dough and mix well.
- Divide the dough into two or three 600g (22oz) pieces. Shape the loaves as desired.
- Stretch each piece into a rectangular roll about 22 x 25cm (9 x 10in). Fold the dried fruits and nuts into the dough, like folding a Swiss roll. Roll tightly to avoid air pockets and shape into a long roll. Make sure that the seams are closed.

Second/final rise   2 hours

- Rise again until almost doubled, about 2 hours at a comfortable room temperature of around 20–25°C (70–80°F). Make sure the dough is covered or mist with water to prevent drying.

Bake

- Preheat oven to 235°C (455°F).
- Bake for about 10 minutes, then reduce the oven to 210°C (410°F) for a further 20–25 minutes for the 600g (22oz) loaves.
- Time for baking will vary. The loaves should be dark brown due to the chocolate powder used in the dough. They must sound hollow when knocked on the bottom.
- If you are unsure whether the loaves have cooked through, turn the oven off, and let the loaves sit in the oven for a further 10 minutes.
- Remove loaves from oven, taking care not to burn yourself!

Rest

- Let the bread cool on a rack before cutting.

Bread is suitable for freezing and will keep for a couple of months frozen.

scrumptious fruit and nut rye and spelt sourdough

This easily is the most beautiful looking bread in cross section. The grey-brown crumb is bejewelled with small bits of nuts and fruits. It tastes as spectacular as it looks. I love this bread, it is incredibly satisfying to have as toast in the morning, slathered with a thick layer of organic butter and a bitter sweet marmalade. It really tastes so good!

scrumptious fruit and nut rye and spelt sourdough

Ingredients

500g (17oz) thin and active rye starter culture

750g (26¹/₂oz) organic wholemeal spelt flour, preferably stone-ground. For a lighter version, substitute half with white spelt flour

100g (3¹/₂oz) unprocessed honey or raw organic sugar

375g (13fl oz) filtered water, room temperature

4 teaspoons (20g) sea salt, finely ground

400g (14oz) dried fruits (such as sultanas, figs, apricots)

150g (5oz) walnuts or pecan

2295g makes two small sandwich loaves (340g/12oz bakers tin)

Method

Measure ingredients
- Using, preferably, a digital scale, weigh all ingredients, including the water. Put all ingredients in a non-metallic bowl, starting with water and starter, flour and then salt last.

Mix ingredients   2–3 mins
- Using a spatula or wooden spoon, stir the ingredients together until they form a cohesive mass.

Rest   15–20 mins
- Rest the dough in the bowl for 15–20 minutes. This step allows the flour to absorb the water.

Kneading—air kneading   5 mins
- This dough is wet and you may find it easier to oil the work surface or bench and your hands.
- Using your fingertips, throw the dough into the air and then slap/throw it onto the bench.
- Repeat this action for about 5 minutes until the dough develops some elasticity.

Rest   20–30 mins
- Rest the dough. As a general rule, 20 minutes rest is sufficient. However, if the dough is still sticky, rest for longer. This step relaxes the gluten and gives the gluten strands a chance to re-align themselves.
- The dough should feel soft, elastic and slightly sticky.

Adjust flour or water (if necessary)
- If after the 30-minute rest period the dough still feels wet or too dry, add more water or flour. I find the best way to do this is to dip your hands in the water or flour and re-knead the dough until it feels right.

Final kneading (if necessasry)   3–5 mins
- If the dough isn't elastic, soft and looking silky smooth, air knead further.
- Do a windowpane test.

Add the fruits and nuts

- Mix the fruit and nuts into the dough well.

Divide and shape   5 mins

- Divide the dough into one or two pieces, depending on the dough quantity.
- Shape the loaves as desired or stretch each piece into a rectangular roll about 22 x 25cm (9 x 10in). Roll tightly to avoid air pockets, like folding a Swiss roll, and shape into a long roll. Make sure that the seams are closed well by pressing them together.

First and final rise   2 hours

- Rise again until almost doubled, about 2 hours at a comfortable room temperature of around 20–25°C (70–80°F). Make sure the dough is covered or mist with water to prevent drying.

Bake

- Preheat the oven to 235°C (455°F) for at least 30 minutes, prepare a water bath in a shallow oven tray and place in the oven.
- Bake the tinned loaves in a hot oven for 12–15 minutes, then reduce the oven to 210°C (410°F) for a further 35–40 minutes until the bread is cooked through and quite dark brown in colour.
- Remove loaves from oven and immediately invert loaves onto a cooling rack, taking care not to burn yourself.
- If you are unsure whether the loaves have cooked through, turn the oven off, and let them sit in the oven for a further 10 minutes.

Rest

- Let the bread cool on a rack before cutting.

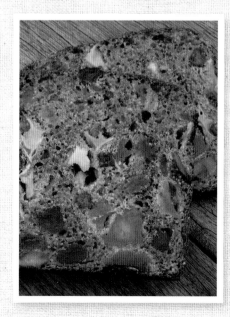

Bread is suitable for freezing and will keep for a couple of months frozen.

apple crumble sourdough tea bread

This bread was created after I made such a huge quantity of apple crumble and there was plenty left over. Surprisingly, it made such a beautiful sourdough bread that I think it is worth making the apple crumble just for the bread. It is not an overly sweet bread and is fragrant with the scent of apple and crunchy bits of oats. You can replace the apple crumble with 350g (12oz) toasted muesli and 150g (5oz) stewed apple.

Ingredients

150g (5oz) rye starter culture

or

150g (5oz) unbleached white spelt starter (ripe and at room temperature), for a lighter bread

500g (18oz) homemade apple crumble

650g (23oz) organic unbleached white wheat or spelt flour

400g (14fl oz) organic apple juice or filtered water, room temperature

3 teaspoons (15g) sea salt, finely ground

―――――――――――――――

1715g (60.5oz) makes 2–3 free-form loaves

Method

Measure ingredients

- Using, preferably, a digital scale, weigh all ingredients, except the apple crumble. Put all ingredients in a non-metallic bowl, starting with water and starter, flour and then salt last.

Mix ingredients   2–3 mins

- Using a spatula or wooden spoon, stir the ingredients together until they form a cohesive mass.

Rest   15–20 mins

- Rest the dough in the bowl for 15–20 minutes. This step allows the flour to absorb the water.

Kneading—air kneading   5 mins

- This dough is wet and you may find it easier to oil the work surface or bench and your hands.
- Using your fingertips, throw the dough into the air and then slap/ throw it onto the bench.
- Repeat this action for about 5 minutes until the dough develops some elasticity.

Rest   20–30 mins

- Rest the dough. As a general rule, 20 minutes rest is sufficient. However, if the dough is still sticky, rest for longer. This step relaxes the gluten and giving the gluten strands a chance to re-align themselves.
- The dough should feel soft, elastic and slightly sticky.

Adjust flour or water (if necessary)

- If after the 30-minute rest period the dough still feels wet or too dry, add more water or flour. I find the best way to do this is to dip your hands in the water or flour and re-knead the dough until it feels right. Do a windowpane test.

Add apple crumble

- Mix the apple crumble or toasted muesli and stewed apple into the dough well.

Divide and shape   5 mins

- Divide the dough into two or three pieces.
- Shape the loaves as desired or stretch each piece into a rectangular roll about 22 x 25cm (9 x 10in). Like folding a Swiss roll, roll tightly to avoid air pockets and shape into a long roll. Make sure that the seams are closed.

First and final rise   2 hours

- Rise again until almost doubled, about 2 hours at a comfortable room temperature of around 20–25°C (70–80°F). Make sure the dough is covered or mist with water to prevent drying.

Bake

- Preheat the oven to 235°C (455°F) for at least 30 minutes.
- Bake the tinned loaves for 12–15 minutes, then reduce the oven to 210°C (410°F) for a further 35–40 minutes until the bread is cooked through and quite dark brown in colour.
- Remove the loaves from the oven, immediately invert them onto a cooling rack, taking care not to burn yourself.
- If you are unsure whether the loaves have cooked through, turn the oven off, and let the loaves sit in the oven for a further 10 minutes.

Rest

- Let the bread cool on a rack before cutting.

Bread is suitable for freezing and will keep for a couple of months frozen.

currant, orange candied peel and fennel rye bread

currant, orange candied peel and fennel rye bread

Ingredients

150g (5oz) rye starter culture

or

150g (5oz) unbleached white spelt starter, for a lighter bread (ripe and at room temperature)

600g (22oz) organic unbleached white wheat or spelt flour

200g (7oz) organic whole-rye flour

450g (16fl oz) filtered water, room temperature

100g (3^1/$_2$oz) orange or kumquat marmalade

3 teaspoons (15g) sea salt, finely ground

To add after the first rise:
2 cups currants

^{1}/$_2$ cup candied orange or cumquat or grapes, finely chopped.

2–3 teaspoon fennel seeds, to taste

Method

Measure ingredients

- Using, preferably, a digital scale, weigh all ingredients, including the water. Put all ingredients in a non-metallic bowl, starting with water and starter, flour and the salt last.

Mix ingredients   2–3 mins

- Using a spatula or wooden spoon, stir the ingredients together until they form a cohesive mass.

Rest   15–20 mins

- Rest the dough in the bowl for 15–20 minutes. This step is most important for wholegrain/wholemeal dough, allowing a greater absorption of water.

Kneading—air kneading   5 mins

- Using your fingertips, throw the dough into the air and then slap/throw it onto the bench. You may find it easier to oil the bench and your hands.
- After you have done this for about 5 minutes, the dough will have developed some elasticity.

Rest   20–30 mins

- Rest the dough. As a general rule, 20 minutes rest is sufficient. However, if the dough is still sticky, rest for longer. This step relaxes the gluten and giving the gluten strands a chance to re-align themselves.
- The dough should feel soft, elastic and slightly sticky.

Adjust flour or water (if necessary)

- If after the 30-minute rest period the dough still feels wet or too dry, add more water or flour. I find the best way to do this is to dip your hands in the water or flour and re-knead the dough until it feels right.

Final kneading (if necessary)   3–5 mins

- If the dough isn't elastic, soft and looks silky smooth, air knead further.
- Do a windowpane test.

- Gather the dough together and try to make a ball. Let it rest in a non-metallic container or bowl covered with a wet tea towel or cling wrap.

First rise   4–6 hours

- Let the dough rise until almost doubled—the time taken will vary.

Divide and shape   5 mins

- Add the cranberry, nuts and bitter chocolate pieces and mix well into the dough.
- Divide the dough into two or three x 600g (22oz) pieces. Shape the loaves as desired.
- Stretch each piece into a rectangular roll about 22 x 25cm (9x 10in). Like folding a Swiss roll, fold the dried fruit into the dough, rolling tightly to avoid air pockets and shape into a long roll. Make sure that the seams are closed well by pressing them together.

Second/final rise   2 hours

- Rise again until almost doubled, about 2 hours at a comfortable room temperature around 20–25°C (70–80°F). Make sure the dough is covered or mist with water to prevent drying.

Bake

- Preheat oven to 235°C (455°F).
- Bake for about 10 minutes, then reduce the oven to 210°C (410°F) for a further 20–25 minutes for the 600g (22oz) loaves.
- Time for baking will vary. They must sound hollow when knocked on the bottom.
- If you are unsure whether the loaves have cooked through, turn the oven off, and let the loaves sit in the oven for a further 10 minutes.
- Remove the loaves from the oven, taking care not to burn yourself!

Rest

- Let the bread cool on a rack before cutting.

Bread is suitable for freezing and will keep for a couple of months frozen.

Pizza, flat breads and crackers

Ciabatta, authentic Italian pizza and turkish bread share two characteristics, crumbs that are full of large air pockets (holes) and a thin crispy crust. To achieve this, you need to increase the proportion of water to flour, creating a wet dough. It takes some practice to handle this wet dough, you need to oil or flour the bench and oil your fingers. There is practically no shaping involved. Once the dough has risen, you simply cut the dough to the size you desire and stretch the dough to create the shape you want. For example, an elongated oval for turkish bread or round shape for pizza.

On the other hand, lavash, chapatti and grizzini dough are somewhat stiffer than a normal dough where the hydration (proportion of water) is reduced slightly to yield a firmer dough that can be easily shaped or rolled thinly.

Baking on a hot (275°C/527°F) preheated granite stone is essential for all pizza, turkish bread and ciabatta. The searing heat will create an oven spring and a crispy crust to help create maximum 'puff', full of large and small air bubbles.

the best sourdough pizza base

After trying many combinations of flours, I find that this combination of unbleached white spelt and unbleached white wheat simply makes the best pizza base. This dough will be slightly stickier than my standard dough to begin with, but after the first rise this dough will become less sticky and 'bubbly' with visible air pockets. This dough produces an authentic italian pizza, a crispy base with large holes, providing you make a thin base and do not overload it with too many ingredients for toppings. See below for topping suggestions. Simplicity is the best here! You can use either wheat or spelt starter culture but I find the best result is achieved using rye starter culture.

Ingredients

6–8 small individual pizza bases:

150g (5oz) rye starter culture (made with 1:1.5 ratio of flour to water)

300g (11oz) organic unbleached white premium bakers flour

300g (11oz) organic unbleached white spelt flour

400ml (14fl oz) filtered water, room temperature

2 teaspoons (10g) sea salt, finely ground

Suggested toppings

- bocconcini, cherry tomatoes, torn fresh basil
- roasted capsicum, fresh goat cheese and basil
- roasted pumpkin, gruyère and pine nuts
- mozzarella, olives and mushroom
- mozzarella, ham, cheese, pickled artichoke

Method

Measure ingredients

- Using, preferably, a digital scale, weigh all ingredients, including the water. Put all ingredients in a non-metallic bowl, starting with water and starter, flour and then salt last.

Mix ingredients   2–3 mins

- Using a spatula or wooden spoon, stir the ingredients together until they form a cohesive mass.

Rest   15–20 mins

- Rest the dough in the bowl for 15–20 minutes. This step allows the absorption of water.

Kneading—air kneading   5 mins

- Using your fingertips, throw the dough into the air and then slap/throw it onto the bench. You may find it easier to oil the bench and your hands.
- After you have done this for about 5 minutes, the dough will have developed some elasticity.

Rest   20–30 mins

- Rest the dough. As a general rule, 20 minutes rest is sufficient. This step relaxes the gluten and gives the gluten strands a chance to re-align themselves.
- The dough should feel soft, elastic and sticky.

Adjust flour or water (if necessary)

- If after the 30-minute rest period the dough still feels too wet, resist adding more flour. This dough will be stickier than others.

Final kneading (if necessary)   3–5 mins

- If the dough isn't elastic, soft and looks silky smooth, air knead further.
- Do a windowpane test.
- Gather the dough together and try to make a ball, let it rest in a covered non-metallic container or a bowl covered with a wet tea towel or cling wrap.

First rise   4–6 hours or overnight

- Let the dough rise until almost doubled—the time taken will vary.

Divide and shape   5 mins

- Divide and shape the dough to 150–200g pieces (5–7oz), then proceed to stretch the dough to a round pizza shape of about 25cm (10in) diameter.
- It is best not to use a rolling pin, but stretch the dough with your fingertips because rolling the dough will de-gas all the beautiful holes that have developed during fermentation, and by doing so you will end up with a flat pizza.
- Use your fingertips to create indentations on the pizza base.

No second/final rise

Baking

- Pre-heated the oven to 275°C (527°F) (bottom heat and fan, no top heat if possible) with a pizza stone or granite tile for at least 30 minutes to create a very hot oven.
- Bake for 3–7 minutes directly on the granite tile or on the bottom part of the oven, and another 5–8 minutes on the top part of the oven until brown.

sourdough ciabatta

This recipe is dedicated to my mother who challenged me to make ciabatta, a flat loaf full of uneven large holes with a crisp crust. The sourdough version is slightly different from the yeasted one. The crumb is chewier, the crust is thicker and the flavour is more complex than its yeasted version.

This wet ciabatta dough is easiest made with a mixer or bread-making machine because this is an extremely sticky dough, and the tendency for most of us is to add more flour as we are kneading it. However, you can hand-knead this by stirring your dough with a large and strong wooden spoon or silicon spatula a few times until it comes together and becomes strechy and elastic (2–3 minutes). Then, tip the bowl onto an oiled bench and with oiled hands, slap the dough onto the bench several times for 2–3 minutes. The minimal kneading will gve you the authentic uneven holes that ciabatta has.

You can add about 100 grams (3.5oz)of salted olives (pitted) to make sourdough olive ciabatta,

sourdough ciabatta

Ingredients

100g (3.5oz) rye starter culture (made with 1:1.5 ratio of flour to water)

500g (18oz) organic unbleached white wheat/spelt or atta flour

375g (13fl oz) filtered water room temperature

2 teaspoons (10g) fine sea salt

1062g (37½oz) makes about 3 small loaves

Method

Measure ingredients

- Using, preferably, a digital scale, weigh all ingredients, including the water. Put all ingredients in a non-metallic bowl, starting with water and starter, flour and the salt last.

Mix ingredients   2–3 mins

- Using a spatula or a wooden spoon, stir the ingredients together until it forms a cohesive mass.

Rest   30 mins

- Rest the dough in the bowl for 30 minutes. This step is most important for a wet dough, like ciabatta, allowing a greater absorption of water.

Stiring and kneading—air kneading   5 mins

- Using a strong and large wooden spoon or spatula, stir your dough inside the bowl about 20–30 times until the dough becomes stretchy and elastic, and it becomes very difficult to stir further, about 2–3 minutes.
- Oil your hands and your bench, tip the wet and sticky dough onto the oiled bench and using your fingertips, throw the dough into the air and then slap/throw it onto the bench.
- After you have done this for 2–3 minutes, the dough will have developed some elasticity.

Rest   30 mins

- Rest the dough. This step relaxes the gluten and gives the gluten strands a chance to re-align themselves.
- The dough should feel soft, elastic and sticky.

Final kneading (if necessary)   3–5 mins

- If the dough isn't elastic, soft and looks silky smooth, air knead further.
- Do a windowpane test.
- Gather the dough together and try to make a ball. Let it rest in a non-metallic container or a bowl covered with a wet tea towel or cling wrap.

First rise   4–6 hours or overnight

- Let the dough rise in the fridge overnight until almost doubled—the time taken will vary.
- The dough will still feel sticky and full of large air bubbles.

Divide and stretch   5 mins

- Invert the risen dough onto a well-floured (semolina is best) bench.
- Sprinkle generous amounts of semolina flour onto the dough.
- Divide the dough with a large dough scraper into 3 pieces then very carefully stretch each piece to about 23–25cm (9–10in) long. Be careful not to destroy the air bubbles.
- No shaping is required here.

Second/final rise   30 mins

- Leave dough on the bench for half an hour to let the gluten rest after being stretched.

Baking

- Pre-heat the oven to 275°C (275°F) (bottom heat and fan, no top heat if possible) with a pizza stone or granite tile in the oven for at least 30 minutes to create a very hot oven.
- Use a water bath on the top rack while baking.
- Bake for 7–8 minutes directly on the granite tile or on the bottom of the oven, then bake for another 5–7 minutes in the top part of the oven until brown.

sourdough Turkish bread

This recipe was created because of my daughter's love for Turkish bread—the soft interior crumb of white chewy bread with a thin crust. The sourdough version is different, it is chewier and has more complex flavour than the white yeasted Turkish bread. You can substitute all of the flours with atta flour or all white flour if you wish.

This is another wet and sticky dough that is better handled by a dough mixer or a breadmaker. However, you can hand-knead this by stirring your dough with a large and strong wooden spoon or silicon spatula a few times until it comes together and becomes strechy and elastic (2–3 minutes). Then, tip the bowl onto an oiled bench, and with oiled hands, slap the dough onto the bench several times (2–3 minutes). The minimal kneading will gve you the authentic uneven holes that Turkish bread has.

You need to use a granite tile that has been pre-heated to 275°C (530°F) in the oven. I use the bottom heat and fan in my oven.

sourdough Turkish bread

Ingredients

150g (5oz) rye starter culture (made with 1:1.5 ratio of flour to water)

650g (23oz) organic flour premium bakers flour

200g (5oz) organic wholemeal or unbleached white spelt flour

650g (23fl oz) filtered water room temperature

3 teaspoons (15g) fine sea salt

1570g (55¹⁄₂oz) makes about 3 loaves

Toppings to be sprinkled before baking:

¹⁄₄ cup sesame seeds (organic)

1 teaspoon black nigella seeds

Method

Measure ingredients

- Using, preferably, a digital scale, weigh all ingredients, including the water. Put all ingredients in a non-metallic bowl, starting with water and starter, flour and the salt last.

Mix ingredients   2–3 mins

- Using a spatula or a wooden spoon, stir the ingredients together until it forms a cohesive mass.

Rest   30 mins

- Rest the dough in the bowl for 30 minutes. This step is most important for a wet dough, like ciabatta, allowing a greater absorption of water.

Stiring and kneading—air kneading   5 mins

- Using a strong and large wooden spoon or spatula, stir your dough in the bowl 20–30 times until the dough becomes stretchy and elastic, and it becomes difficult to stir further.
- Oil your hands and the bench, tip the wet and sticky dough onto the bench. Using your fingertips, throw the dough into the air and then slap/throw it onto your bench.
- After you have done this for about 2–3 minutes, the dough will have developed some elasticity.

Rest   30 mins

- Rest the dough. This step relaxes the gluten and giving the gluten strands a chance to re-align themselves.
- The dough should feel soft, elastic and sticky.

Final kneading (if necessary)   3–5 mins

- If the dough isn't elastic, soft and looks silky smooth, air knead further.
- Do a windowpane test.
- Gather the dough together and try to make a ball, let it rest in a non-metallic container or a bowl covered with a wet tea towel or cling wrap.

First rise   4–6 hours or overnight

- Let the dough rise until almost doubled—the time taken will vary.
- The dough will still feel sticky and full of large air bubbles.

Divide and stretch   5 mins

- Invert the risen dough onto a well-floured bench.
- Sprinkle generous amounts of flour onto the dough.
- Divide the dough with a large dough scraper into two or three pieces then; very carefully so as not to destroy the air bubbles, proceed to stretch the dough to long rectangles of about 20 x 35cm (10 x 12in) diameter.
- It is best not to use a rolling pin, but stretch the dough with your fingertips because rolling the dough will de-gas all the beautiful holes that have developed during fermentation, and by doing so you will end up with a flat Turkish bread.
- Use your fingertips to create indentations and sprinkle generously with the seeds. Nigella seeds have a strong and pungent taste, use them judiciously.

Second/final rise

- Leave the dough on the bench for half an hour to let the gluten rest after being stretched.

Baking

- Pre-heat the oven to 275°C (525°F). Set the bottom heat and fan, no top heat, if possible, for at least 30 minutes to create a very hot oven with a pizza stone or granite tile.
- Use a water bath on the top shelf of the oven.
- Bake for 5 minutes directly on the granite tile or on the bottom part of the oven and another 10 minutes on the top part of the oven until brown.

sourdough chapatti

Chapatti is one of the most common Indian breads. It is small, flat, round bread, traditionally made with atta flour (or sifted wholemeal flour). Each bread is cooked individually on a hot griddle or cast iron pan until it is partially cooked and blistered with brown spots, then it is finished by exposing it to an open flame. Once cooked, you have the option to brush the chapatti with melted butter or ghee. This is a stiff dough, unlike other doughs in this book.

Ingredients

100g (3½oz) white starter culture (made with 1:1 ratio of flour to water)

400g (14oz) atta flour or sifted wholemeal flour

200g (7fl oz) filtered water, room temperature

1 teaspoon (5g) fine sea salt

705g (25oz) makes about 15 chapattis

Optional:
melted butter or ghee for brushing after each chapatti is cooked.

Method

Measure ingredients

• Using, preferably, a digital scale, weigh all ingredients, including the water. Put all ingredients in a non-metallic bowl, starting with water and starter, flour and the salt last.

Mix ingredients   2–3 mins

• Using a spatula or wooden spoon, stir the ingredients together until they form a cohesive mass.

Rest   15–20 mins

• Rest the dough in the bowl for 15–20 minutes. This step is most important for wholegrain/wholemeal dough, allowing a greater absorption of water.

Kneading—air kneading   5 mins

• Using your fingertips, throw the dough into the air and then slap/throw it onto the bench. You may find it easier to oil the bench and your hands.

• After you have done this for about 5 minutes, the dough will have developed some elasticity.

Rest   20–30 mins

• Rest the dough. As a general rule, 20 minutes rest is sufficient.

• The dough should feel soft, elastic and not sticky at all.

• Final kneading (if necessary)   3–5 mins
- If the dough isn't elastic, soft and looks silky smooth, air knead further.
- Do a windowpane test.
- Gather the dough together and try to make a ball, let it rest in a non-metallic container or a bowl covered with a wet tea towel or cling wrap.

First rise   4 hours
- Let the dough rise until almost doubled—the time taken will vary.

Divide and shape   5 mins
- Divide the dough with a large dough scraper into about 15–18 portions. Roll each piece into a ball.
- Set the griddle or cast iron skillet pan onto the stove to heat up.
- Using a small rolling pin, roll each piece until a round disk of 5cm (2in), dust with more flour on both sides. Then roll again until it is thin and about 15cm (6in) in diameter. Slap the chapatti between your palms to remove excess flour

Baking
- Check the griddle is very hot before you slip the chapatti onto it.
- Cook for one minute until small bubbles start to form on the top surface.
- Flip onto the other side, small brown spots will be visible on this side. Cook on this flipside for another half-minute or so.
- Take the griddle off the heat to avoid over heating.
- Turn up the gas flame to high.
- Using a long thong (with a silicon handle, so as not to burn your hand), place the chapatti directly over the flame. Within 10–15 seconds the chapatti will expand and puff into a balloon.
- Flip to the other side at once for a few seconds until it is blistered with brown flecks, then remove from the flame immediately.
- Brush with melted butter or ghee and keep warm and covered on a plate.
- Eat immediately!

sourdough lavash
or crisp cracker bread

As far as I am aware, traditional crisp cracker breads from all over the world are unleavened—no yeast added—whether it is sourdough starter or commercial yeast.

Here I have created my own version of crisp cracker bread/lavash, using a fair amount of sourdough starter. The reason for this is 'digestibility'. As you know by now, sourdough starters pre-digest the gluten and eliminate phytic acids, rendering these crackers full of nutrients for you, as well as being somewhat more-ish on their own or with a myriad of dips (I've included some dip recipes in the last chapter of this book).

Note: This is a stiff dough, similar to a pasta dough, which you can put through a pasta machine to create thin sheets for making crackers.

Ingredients

200g (7oz) white starter culture (made with 1:1 ratio of flour to water)

90–100g (3–3.5fl oz) filtered water, room temperature

75g ($2\frac{1}{2}$oz) semolina flour

200g (7oz) whole wheat flour

1 teaspoon (5g) sea salt, finely ground

575g (20oz) makes about 6 long, sheet crackers

Note: You can make a wheat-free version by using kamut flur and spelt flour instead of semolina flour and wheat flour.

Method

Measure ingredients

- Using, preferably, a digital scale, weigh all ingredients, including the water. Put all ingredients in a non-metallic bowl, starting with water and starter, flour and then salt last.

Mix ingredients   2–3 mins

- Using a spatula or wooden spoon, stir the ingredients together until they form a cohesive mass.

Rest   30 mins

- Rest the dough in the bowl for 30 minutes. This step allows the semolina flour to absorb the water.

Kneading—air kneading   5 mins

- Using your fingertips, throw the dough into the air and then slap/throw it onto the bench.
- Repeat this action for about 5 minutes, until the dough develops some elasticity.

Rest   20–30 mins

- Rest the dough for another 30 minutes. This step relaxes the gluten and gives the gluten strands a chance to re-align themselves.
- The dough should feel soft and elastic

Final kneading (if necessary)   3–5 mins

- If the dough isn't elastic, soft and looks silky smooth, air knead further.
- Do a windowpane test.

First rise

- Scoop all the dough back into the oiled bowl.
- Let rise covered with a wet tea towel or cling wrap for about 2 hours. The dough will rise by 30–50 per cent.

Shape

- Dust the bench generously with semolina flour, invert the dough onto the bench.
- Divide the dough into 10 or 12 pieces (approx. 100–150g each), round each piece gently with your hand to form small balls.
- Rest for about half an hour to relax the gluten.
- Roll each ball into a 20cm (8in) elongated sausage shape.
- Using the instruction of the pasta maker, feed each piece into the pasta machine as though you were making a lasagna sheet. Roll a few on each setting, starting with the maximum setting until you get to the number 3–4 thickness setting.
- Stretch the 'lasagna sheet' into the desired shape, cut in half if necessary to fit onto the granite stone top.
- Place each cracker on a parchment/baking paper.

Bake

- Pre-heat the oven to 250°C (480°F), at least 30–45 minutes before baking.
- Bake the cracker sheet (on the baking paper) directly on the hot granite stone for about 5–10 minutes until golden and crisp.
- The cracker will puff up and stay puff up.
- Remove the cracker sheet from the oven, taking care not to burn yourself!

Best eaten on the day or keep in an airtight container for a week.

sourdough sesame grissini

Grissini, the commonly known Italian breadsticks, are almost indispensable in any antipasto platter. They are crunchy and slightly salty, often they are sprinkled with sesame seeds for extra crunch and flavour.

This is a stiff dough to allow you to roll and shape the dough into bread sticks.

Note: *Lower heat is used here, to dry the breadsticks and create maximum crunch all the way through the bread sticks.*

sourdough sesame grissini

Ingredients

250g (9oz) white starter culture (made with 1:1 ratio of flour to water)

350g (12oz) atta flour

150g (5oz) fine semolina flour

225g (8fl oz) filtered water

or

300g (11oz) rye starter culture (made with 1:1.5 ratio of flour to water)

200g (7oz) white spelt flour

150g (5oz) wholemeal spelt flour

200g (7oz) kamut flour

250g (9fl oz) filtered water

Add 70g (2½oz) of sesame seeds, half way through kneading for both recipes.

Extra sesame seeds for rolling each grissini

1070g makes about 15 grissini sticks

Method

Measure ingredients
- Using, preferably, a digital scale, weigh all ingredients, including the water. Put all ingredients in a non-metallic bowl, starting with water and starter, flour and then salt last.

Mix ingredients   2–3 mins
- Using a spatula or wooden spoon, stir the ingredients together until they form a cohesive mass.

Rest   10–20 mins
- Rest the dough in the bowl for up to 20 minutes. This step allows the semolina/kamut flour to absorb the water.

Kneading—air kneading   5 mins
- Using your fingertips, throw the dough into the air and then slap/throw it onto the bench.
- Repeat this action for about 5 minutes until the dough develops some elasticity.

Rest   20–30 mins
- Rest the dough for another 30 minutes. This step relaxes the gluten and gives the gluten strands a chance to re-align themselves.
- The dough should feel soft and elastic.

• Adjust flour or water (if necessary)
- If after the 30-minute rest period the dough still feels wet, add more flour. I find the best way to do this is to dip your hands in the flour and re-knead the dough until it feels right.

Final kneading (if necessary)   3–5 mins
- If the dough isn't elastic, soft and looks silky smooth, air knead further.
- Do a windowpane test.

First rise

- Scoop all the dough back into the oiled bowl.
- Let rise covered with a wet tea towel or cling wrap for about 2 hours. The dough will rise by 30–50 per cent.

Shape

- Dust the bench generously with semolina and invert the dough onto the bench.
- Divide the dough into 10 or 12 pieces (100–150g each), round each piece gently with your hand to form small balls.
- Rest for about half an hour to relax the gluten.
- Roll each ball into a 20cm (8in) elongated sausage shape.
- Using the instruction of the pasta maker, feed each piece into the pasta machine as though you were making a lasagna sheet. Roll a couple on each setting, starting with the maximum setting, until you get to the number 3–4 thickness setting.
- Stretch the 'lasagna sheet' into the desired shape, cut in half if necessary to fit onto the granite stone top.
- Place each cracker on parchment/baking paper.

Bake

- Pre-heat the oven to 150°C (300°F), at least 30–45 minutes before baking.
- Bake the cracker sheet (on the baking paper) directly on the hot granite stone for about 30–45 minutes until golden and crisp.
- The cracker will puff up and stay puffeded up.
- Remove the cracker sheet from the oven, taking care not to burn yourself!

Best eaten on the day or keep in an airtight container for a week.

authentic sourdough boiled bagels

I love bagels, but only the real boiled bagel will do for me and my family. It is the chewy sweetness that makes real boiled bagels taste so sublime and moorish. Here I want to show you that bagels are so easy to make in your home kitchen. In fact, it is an experience best shared with your children and/or loved ones, because you are going to need more than a pair of hands to shape, cook and bake the bagels.

The dough is fairly stiff, making it easier to handle and shape, suitable for getting your kids involved in rolling and shaping the bagels. Bagels freeze well, so it is well worth the effort to make a double batch to save you more cleaning and washing up.

Ingredients

300g (11oz) thin and active
white starter culture
(made with 1:1 flour to water ratio)

250g (9fl oz) filtered water, room
temperature

275g organic atta flour

275g unbleached white wheat flour
(premium bakers flour)

3 teaspoons (15g) sea salt,
finely ground

1065g makes 8–10 bagels

Method

Measure ingredients

- Using, preferably, a digital scale, weigh all ingredients, including the water. Put all ingredients in a non-metallic bowl, starting with water and starter, flour and then salt last.

Mix ingredients   2–3 mins

- Using a spatula or wooden spoon, stir the ingredients together until they form a cohesive mass.

Rest   10–20 mins

- Rest the dough in the bowl for 10–20 minutes. This step allows the semolina flour to absorb the water.

Kneading—air kneading   5 mins

- Using your fingertips, throw the dough into the air and then slap/throw it onto the bench.
- Repeat this action for about 5 minutes until the dough develops some elasticity.

Rest   20–30 mins

- Rest the dough for another 30 minutes. This step relaxes the gluten and gives the gluten strands a chance to re-align themselves.
- The dough should feel soft, elastic, stiff and fairly sticky.

Final kneading (if necessary)   3–5 mins

- If the dough isn't elastic, soft and looks silky smooth, air knead further.
- Do a windowpane test.

First rise   2–3 hours

- Scoop all the dough back into the oiled bowl.
- Let rise covered with a wet tea towel or wet cling wrap for about 2 hours. The dough will rise by 30–50 per cent.

Shape   10 mins

- Dust the bench generously with semolina flour, invert the dough onto the bench.
- Divide the dough into 8–10 pieces (100–150g each). Round each piece gently with your hand to form small balls.
- Rest for about half an hour to relax the gluten.
- Roll each ball into a 20cm (8in) elongated sausage shape.
- Join the two ends together, then slot your fingers into the hole. Apply a gentle pressure on the joint, and roll the joint together to create a seal. Now you have the authentic 'bagel' ring shape.
- Dust two baking trays and each bagel generously with semolina flour, and place them 2cm (1in) apart on the baking tray.

Final rise   2 hours

- Let the dough rise again for another 2 hours until it has increased in size by 50 per cent. Do not over-rise.

Bake   30 mins

- Preheat the oven to 235°C (455°F) for about 30 minutes.
- Fill a large wok or wide-mouthed saucepan (26–28cm diameter) with water.
- If you like, you can add a tablespoon of liquid malt into the water to give the bagel its characteristic malty crust.
- Boil the water until it has come to a rolling boil, then reduce the heat to keep it on a simmer (small bubbles appearing in the water).
- While the water is simmering, increase the heat to medium. Gently drop 2–3 bagels with a large round slotted spoon into the simmering water.
- Using the slotted spoon to flip the bagels, 'poach' the bagel in the water for about 30 seconds on each side.
- Remove the bagels carefully with the slotted spoon, draining off all of the water before placing them onto a parchment paper-lined baking tray.
- Bake the bagels (on the tray) on the granite at the bottom of a 235°C (455°F) preheated oven for about 10 minutes, until golden brown.
- Remove bagels from oven, taking care not to burn yourself!

Bagels are suitable for freezing and will keep for a couple of months frozen.

Sourdough cakes

It is easy to find many great recipes for sourdough cakes both in print media and on the internet. However, those recipes include either baking powder or baking soda and, more often than not, both in large quantities. These two self-raising agents/chemicals serve two purposes: to neutralise the acidity of the sourdough starter and to rise the cakes. However, by adding those ingredients you lose all the benefit of the lactic acid fermentation, that is, the digestibility (of gluten) and nutrients is compromised.

I am a purist and believe that sourdough starter helps food to be more digestible and nutrient ready for the body. So, after some experimenting I have created these cake recipes. Even the biggest and loudest critics in my households and innocent bystanders have not been able to detect the distinctive sour taste or smell of the sourdough starter.

In fact, I have found that any of these cakes can be truly vegan by substituting melted butter with mild oil, such as rice bran or grapeseed oil—both can withstand high temperatures without breaking down.

sourdough chocolate cake or cupcakes iced with dark chocolate ganache

This cake is yummy and chocolatey without being sickly sweet or rich. I love to ice it with a dark chocolate ganache or chocolate icing. My 10-year-old daughter who has such a sensitive palate and is a chocoholic, cannot even trace the sourdough taste in it. This is our favourite chocolate cake. It is so easy, you could mix it in your sleep! The mixing should not take any more than 3 minutes or your cake will be tough.

Ingredients

200g (7oz) organic unbleached white wheat or spelt plain flour

50g (2oz) best quality cocoa powder

300g (11oz) organic raw castor sugar

1$\frac{1}{2}$ teaspoon vanilla extract

75g (2$\frac{1}{2}$oz) apple, finely grated

100g (3$\frac{1}{2}$oz) melted butter

200g (7oz) unbleached white wheat or spelt starter (made with 1:1 flour to water ratio)

2 organic eggs

$\frac{1}{2}$ teaspoon sea salt, finely ground

Makes one cake measuring 7 x 11cm (2 x 4in) and 8cm (2$\frac{1}{2}$in) depth

Method

- Prepare the tin: line the bottom and sides of 7 x 11cm (2 x 4in) and 8cm (2$\frac{1}{2}$in) deep baking tin.

Measure ingredients

- In a non-metallic bowl, mix the flour, cocoa and sugar together.
- Add the cooled melted butter and starter.
- Beat the eggs or cream (if using) with salt until fluffy, then tip it into the bowl.

Mix ingredients   2–3 mins

- Using a hand-held beater or kitchen-aid with a paddle, mix the ingredients together until they are thoroughly combined.
- Do not be tempted to over-mix—overmixing will produce a tough cake.

First and final rise   4–6 hours

- Pour the cake batter into the lined tin and cover with a wet tea towel or cling wrap.
- Let the cake rise until it is about 125 per cent larger than its original size. This will take a while and the time taken will vary. In my cool kitchen, about 20–23°C (70–80°F), it took 6 hours for my cake to rise. Most of the rising (increasing volume) will happen during baking. Do not be alarmed if it looks like it hasn't risen at all.

Bake

- Preheat oven to 200°C (390°F).
- Place a water bath in the oven while baking.
- Bake for about 15 minutes, then reduce the oven to 180°C (360°F) for a further hour and fifteen minutes.
- The cake will double, become domed-shape and crack in the oven. Check its done by inserting a wooden bamboo stick into the centre of the cake. It should come out clean.
- Remove the cake from the oven, taking care not to burn yourself!

Rest

- Let the cake cool for 5–10 minutes before inverting.
- Ice with the chocolate ganache while it is still warm, if you wish.
- If you are going to freeze the cake, do not ice it with the chocolate ganache.

Chocolate ganache

- Melt 200g (7oz) of dark chocolate with 200g of cream or 200g of butter. Mix well and spread over cooled cake.

Cake is suitable for freezing and will keep for a couple of months frozen, un-iced.

sourdough gingerbread cake

I am a ginger lover and this cake tastes like the old-fashioned gingerbread cake without the acrid taste and smell of baking soda. The mollases sugar gives the cake the moist chewiness, which is so characteristic of old-world gingerbread cake. This moist cake will keep well for a week or two wrapped in waxed paper.

Ingredients

60g (2oz) melted butter

200g (7oz) golden syrup

100g (3½oz) organic molasses sugar or dark brown sugar or rapadura sugar

150g (5oz) organic raw caster sugar

175g (6oz) organic unbleached white wheat or spelt plain flour

175g (6oz) unbleached white wheat or spelt starter (made with 1:1 flour to water ratio)

1 organic egg

Makes one cake measuring 7 x 11cm (2 x 4in) and 8cm (2½in) depth

Method

• Line the bottom and sides of a deep baking tin.

Measure ingredients

• Over a pan of simmering water, melt the butter and golden syrup in a glass mixing bowl, then add the sugars. Take the bowl out of the pan.

Mix ingredients   2–3 mins

• Add the flour, starter ginger powder and mixed spice powder to the warm mixture.
• Beat the egg or cream (if using) with salt until fluffy, then tip it into the bowl.
• Using a hand-held beater or kitchen-aid fitted with a paddle, mix the ingredients together until they are combined.
• Do not be tempted to over mix—over mixing will produce a tough cake.

First and final rise   4–6 hours

• Pour the cake batter into the fully lined tin and cover the surface with a wet tea towel or cling wrap.
• Let the cake batter rise, covered, until it has risen about 125 per cent. This will take a while and the time taken will vary. There will be a small number of air bubbles on the surface of the cake. In my cool kitchen, about 20–23°C (70–80°F) it took 10 hours for my cake to rise. Most of the rising (increasing volume) will happen during baking. Do not be alarmed if it looks like it hasn't risen at all.

Bake

- Preheat oven to 200°C (390°F).
- Place a water bath in the oven while baking.
- Bake for about 15 minutes, then reduce the oven to 180°C (360°F) for a further hour and fifteen minutes.
- The cake will double in size, dome and crack while baking.
- Check the cake is done by inserting a wooden bamboo stick into the centre of the cake. Itt should come out clean.
- Remove the cake from oven, taking care not to burn yourself!

Rest

- Let the cake cool for about 10 minutes before inverting.

Cake is suitable for freezing and will keep for a couple of months frozen.

sourdough christmas cake

Christmas is a time to celebrate with our loved ones, and what better way to share this joyous time than sharing the making and eating of festive food. It is so much nicer to be given or to eat lovingly prepared home-baked cakes and breads, than store-bought ones.

During Christmas, most of us will suffer from over indulgence of food. However, it is great to know that these traditional Christmas goodies can be made with sourdough starter—thereby increasing the digestibility of these 'rich' food. Lacto-fermentation in sourdough pre-digests the fat, protein and sugar for you. Traditional English Christmas cake is a dense butter cake enriched with fruits, nuts and liqueur, leavened with baking powder. Here we use the sourdough starter as a leavening agent, without the addition of bicarbonate soda or baking powder. The cake will not be light and airy, but it will be dense and complex in flavour—which is what you would want for an exceptional (and easy-to-digest) Christmas cake.

The method is quite simple, just like making any butter cake, the white sourdough starter is added at the end of the mixing before the addition of fruits and nuts.

This Christmas cake batter will not double—it will increase to 1½ times its original size, hence its dense texture.

Ingredients

Fruit and liqueur mixture
Prepare this mixture the day before you plan to make the cake

500g (18oz) a mixture of sultanas, raisins/muscat and currants

50–100g (1.7–3½oz) candied peels (candied orange)

100g (3½oz) pre-soaked, slow-roasted nuts of your choice (pecans, almonds, walnuts) Roast at 70°C (155°F) for 7–10 hours

100ml (3½fl oz) brandy or whisky or any other liqueur of your liking.

Mix well and marinate all above ingredients overnight.

Flour and spice mixture
350g (12oz) organic unbleached white wheat or spelt flour (low gluten), choose plain or cake flour

1½ cups white sourdough starter (made with 1:1 flour and water)

1½ teaspoons mixed spice

½ teaspoon ground cinnamon

½ teaspoon ground ginger or cloves

50g (2oz) ground almonds/almond meal

Sift together all except ground almonds. Mix ground almond into the sifted flour mixture

Butter mixture
300g (11oz) organic butter

200g (7oz) organic caster or icing sugar

100g (3½oz) dark muscovado sugar or dark brown sugar

½ teaspoon sea salt

5 large organic eggs

Method

- Preheat oven to 180°C (360°F).
- Beat butter, sugar and salt until light and fluffy, slowly add the eggs, one by one. The mixture will look curdled at this stage, do not worry!
- Using a spatula or low-speed mixer, add the flour mixture and 1½ cups of white sourdough starter. Mix well.
- Continue to use a spatula, add the fruits and nuts until they are evenly distributed.
- Ferment the dough for approximately 6 hours or overnight (in summer). The dough will increase to about 1½ times its original size.
- Divide the dough into two 18cm (7in) diameter round tins or one 26–28cm (10–11in) tin.
- Bake the cake for 10–15 minutes on the lower third rack, then reduce heat to 150°C (300°F) and bake for 1–1½ hours until golden brown. If the top of the cake browns too quickly, cover with aluminium foil.
- As the cake comes out of the oven, brush generously with the liqueur of your choice. Repeat this several times in the next month, this will ensure the cake is moist and develops its complex taste.
- This cake is best eaten after a month or two when it has developed its complex flavour. It will keep wrapped tightly in waxed paper and aluminium foil and in the coolest part of your house for a month or two. Alternatively, it will keep in the fridge or freeze well for up to 3 months.

Sourdough pastry

olive oil spelt pastry—a dairy-free alternative

Ingredients

50g (2oz) of any sourdough starter

310g (11oz) wholemeal spelt flour

85g (3oz) water or for sweet pastry use maple syrup

75ml (2¹/₂fl oz) extra virgin olive oil—about ¹/₃ cup

1 teaspoon sea salt

Method

• Preheat oven to 200°C (390°F).

• Line a 26cm (10in) pie tin with baking paper or oil.

• Mix ingredients with a spatula/large knife to form a rough mass of dough.

• Press the pastry dough into the pie tin.

• Using a sharp fork, poke holes on the bottom and sides of the pie crust. Chill 30 minutes to 1 hour.

• Bake blind in oven for 10 minutes.

• Pie crust is now ready for filling.

Note: This pie crust will also work without blind baking—you can fill it straight away with roasted vegetables and custard filling.

roasted vegetable tart

You need one quantity of spelt pastry for 26cm (10in) diameter tart tin.

Ingredients

Slow-Roasted Vegetables

800g (30oz) vegetables of your choice, eg. sweet potato, zucchini, aubergine, fennel, pumpkin

3 tablespoons of extra virgin olive oil

1–2 tablespoons balsamic vinegar

A few sprigs of thyme or sage

A pinch of salt flakes of your choice

Caramelised Onions

300g (11oz) onions, cut in half and slice 0.25 cm (¹⁄₁₀in) thin

3 tablespoons of extra virgin olive oil

1 tablespoon balsamic vinegar

1 tablespoon rapadura or brown sugar

A pinch of salt flakes of your choice

Savoury Custard

300g (11oz) or 6 large eggs

200g (7oz) the best cream you can afford (single cream)

¹⁄₄ teaspoon freshly grated nutmeg

1 teaspoon (5g) of salt flakes, or to taste

Freshly ground pepper (optional)

1–2 cloves of roasted garlic

2 teaspoons self-raising flour (optional)—this will make the custard set to a firmer consistency

Method

- Preheat oven to 200°C (390°F) for 30 minutes.
- Cut vegetables into large chunks (remember vegetables will cook for a long time and will shrink).
- Mix the vegetables with the rest of the ingredients, place all in a large baking tin.
- Bake in the hot oven for 10 minutes, then turn the oven off.
- Leave to slow bake for a few hours until the oven cools.

or

- Bake in a preheated oven 180°C (360°F) for 30 minutes.

Method

- In a heavy base frypan heat the extra virgin olive oil. Add the onions and sauté over medium heat for a few minutes until the onions start to soften.
- Add the vinegar, sugar and salt.
- Angle a lid on the frypan to allow steam to escape, reduce the heat to low and continue cooking for 30–40 minutes, stirring from time to time to prevent burning.
- Cook until the onion is soft, caramelised and not too brown.

Method

- Preheat oven to 180°C (350°F).
- Beat the eggs in a large mixing bowl until white and fluffy.
- Pour in the cream and the rest of the ingredients, whisk until well combined.
- Place the mixing bowl in the oven and cook for 35–50 minutes.
- Do not overcook custard, it still needs to look 'wobbly' out of the oven. It will become firmer as it cools.

Enriched dough

Brioche, panettone, stollen, challah and kugelhopf belong to the family of enriched doughs. These enriched doughs are sourdough when the water has been substituted with milk or eggs. Butter and sugar is added to change the flavour and texture of these baked goods.

Panettone, the traditional Italian Christmas cake is essentially a brioche dough, in which dried fruits, sugar and liqueur have been added. Its texture is quite 'light' and airy. The sourdough version is a little denser than the commercial yeasted ones.

sourdough brioche

The biggest challenge for making sourdough brioche is to create a light and airy texture—we achieve this by 'over-kneading' the dough, resulting in a 'fluid' dough. It is a technique that is best suited for machine kneading using a planetary mixer (where the beater rotates), a breadmaker or better still, a spiral mixer (where the bowl rotates—less heat is created).

Ingredients

1kg (35½oz) organic unbleached white wheat/spelt flour (high gluten)

200g (7oz) organic caster or icing sugar

5 large organic eggs

5 large organic egg yolks

100ml (3½fl oz) organic milk (do not use raw milk here, as raw milk contains a milk protein that attacks gluten)

400g (14oz) sourdough milk starter (see Pain de Mie recipe on page 72)

300–500g (10.5–17oz) butter (soft but chilled to touch)

1½ tablespoons salt

You can add as little as 300g or as much as 500g of butter

Traditional brioche uses 50 per cent butter to flour ratio

Method

Mix ingredients

- Using a dough mixer with the dough hook, comine the ingredients and knead for about 5 minutes until the dough comes together.

Rest

- Rest the dough for 20–30 minutes to let the gluten develop.

Add more ingredients

- Add 50g (2oz) melted and cooled cocoa butter.
- Knead dough for a further 10 minutes until you have an elastic dough.
- Rest again for a further 20 minutes.
- Slowly add 300–500g (11–18oz) soft but still chilled butter. Add small blobs of butter to the dough slowly while the machine is running. Continue kneading with the machine until you get a shiny and very elastic dough. The dough will look almost like a shiny, stretchy, elastic—but it is not sticky due to the high butter content. The total kneading time will be 20–30 minutes. This dough needs to be well kneaded to develop the gluten. This is one of those doughs that needs a machine to knead it well, although you could try kneading by hand using a strong wooden spatula.

Rest

- Ferment the dough for approximately 4–6 hours. The dough will increase to about 1½ times its original size.

Shape

- Divide and shape the dough—fill with cheese, chocolate etc., as desired.
- Let the dough double for approximately 5–6 hours.

Bake

- Preheat oven to 230°C (446°F).
- For a 600–800g (22–28oz) brioche, bake the brioche for 10–15 minutes on the lower third rack, then reduce heat to 185°C (365°F) for 30–35 minutes until golden brown.
- For muffin-sized brioche, bake for 5 minutes on the lower third rack, then reduce heat to 185°C (365°F) for 15 minutes until golden brown. If the top browns too quickly, cover with aluminium foil.
- As the brioche comes out of the oven, brush generously with melted ghee or butter. Repeat this process a couple more times as the brioche cools. This helps the brioche to remain soft and moist.
- Brioche freezes well due to its high fat content—up to 3 months. Thaw overnight, then warm in a 200°C (390°F) oven for 10 minutes until warmed through.

sourdough panettone

Panettone is the traditional Italian Christmas cake. Panettone is essentially an enriched brioche dough embelished with dried sultanas or golden raisins, candied citrus peels (both candied orange and traditionally green candied citron) and aromatic essences or liqueurs. My preferred aromatics are a mixture of cointreau, marsala (an Italian 'sherry') and vanilla extract or vanilla bean.

Most panettone is made with commercial yeast, although there has been a revival in Italy for making panettone the traditional way with wild yeast augmented with a small addition of commercial yeast. Italian bakers have discovered that the 'sourdough' panettone has a better shelf life due to its acidity and a more complex taste, which is preferred by customers.

Ingredients

Fruit and liqueur mixture

Prepare this mixture the day before you plan to make the panettone dough.

300g (11oz) sultanas
(or up to 500g (18oz),
if you like more fruit)

200g (7oz) candied peels (candied orange and candied citron—see page 214 for recipe)

1/3 cup marsala

1/4 cup Cointreau

2 tablespoons vanilla extract or seeds from 1–2 large vanilla bean

Mix well and marinate all ingredients overnight.

Dough

1000g (35¹/₂oz) unbleached white wheat/spelt flour (high gluten)

250g (9oz) sugar

5 large organic eggs

5 large organic egg yolks

100ml (3¹/₂fl oz) milk

400g (14oz) sourdough milk starter (see Pain de Mie recipe on page 72)

300g (10.5oz) butter, soft but chilled

50g (2oz) cocoa butter, melted and cooled (optional)

1¹/₂ tablespoons salt

Method

- Use a dough mixer with the dough hook, combine all ingredients and knead for about 5 minutes until the dough comes together. Rest for 20–30 minutes to let the gluten develop.
- Add 50g (2oz) melted and cooled cocoa butter. Knead for a further 10 minutes until you have an elastic dough. Rest again for a further 20 minutes.
- Slowly add 300g (11oz) of soft, but still chilled, butter. Add small blobs of butter to the dough slowly while the machine is running. Continue kneading with the machine until you get a shiny and very elastic dough. It will look almost like a shiny, stretchy, elastic—but it is not sticky due to the high butter content.
- The total kneading time will be approximately 20–30 minutes. Like brioche, this dough needs to be well kneaded to develop the gluten. This is one of those doughs that needs a machine to knead it well, although you could try kneading by hand using a strong spatula.
- Add the fruits and knead them in by hand or machine on low speed until they are evenly distributed.
- Ferment the dough for 4–6 hours. The dough will increase to about 1½ times its original size.
- Divide and shape the dough. This recipe will make about 3 small panettone of 18cm (7in) diameter and about 10cm (4in) high, or about 20 large muffin-sized panettone of about 6.5cm (2½in) diameter.
- Let the dough double, approx. 5–6 hours.

Bake

- Preheat oven to 230°C (446°F).
- Bake the panettone for 10–15 minutes on the lower third rack of the oven, then reduce heat to 185°C (365°F) and bake for a further 30–35 minutes until darkish brown. If the top browns too quickly, cover the top with aluminium foil.
- For muffin size panettone, bake for 5 minutes on the lower third rack, then reduce heat to 185°C (365°F). Bake for a further 15–20 minutes until darkish brown. The dough will almost triple in size in the oven.
- As the panettone comes out of the oven, brush generously with melted ghee or butter mixed with a liqueur of your choice (I recommend a mixture of Cointreau and brandy). Repeat this process as many times as you like because this help the panettone to keep well and moist.

Rest

- Let the panettone cool completely before eating, allow at least 2–3 hours cooling period. Panettone is best eaten within 2 weeks of baking because it will dry out.

Panettone will keep well wrapped tightly in waxed paper and aluminium foil. Left in the coolest part of your house it should keep well for a month or two (I have kept many panettone for 10–12 weeks in winter time). Alternatively, panettone freezes well for 3 months.

Things to go with sourdough

cumquat and Cointreau marmalade

This is a fabulous cumquat marmalade recipe. It is based on a recipe given to me by one of my students, Fran Rieussett. Thank you, Fran!

Ingredients

1000g (35½oz) cumquats, whole

1500ml (51fl oz) water

900–1250g (32–44oz) raw sugar, to taste

juice of 3 lemons (medium–large), optional

5 tablespoons Cointreau

2 vanilla beans (optional) split in half and seeds scraped

Method

- Cut cumquats in half and remove all seeds. Put seeds in a muslin bag or a muslin cloth, tie a knot.
- Place the cumquats and seed bag in a non-reactive 26–32cm (10–12½in) diameter saucepan and cover with water for 24 hours.
- Squeeze all gel-like (pectin) substance from the seed bag into the water.
- Bring all ingredients to a rapid boil.
- Simmer for about one hour, covered.
- Remove muslin bag from the saucepan and again squeeze all the gel-like substance (pectin) from the bag.
- Add all of the sugar and lemon juice, if using.
- Bring all to a rapid boil for about 25–35 minutes. Do a gel test by putting a small amount of the liquid on a cold plate (that has been cooled in the freezer). The marmalade is ready if it gels on the plate.
- Add Cointreau and quickly put marmalade into jars. Leave about a 1cm (½in) gap from the top and close the lid tightly.

fig preserve infused with vanilla bean

Fig preserve is one of my favourite preserves; cooking figs really intensifies the flavour. I have included vanilla beans to add their sumptuous fragrance to the preserve. If you like, you can omit the vanilla beans and add 150–200g of candied or stem ginger about 5 minutes after you add the sugar and lemon juice.

Ingredients

1000g (35^1/$_2$oz) fresh figs, quartered

750g (26^1/$_2$) raw sugar, to taste

juice of 2 lemons (medium–large),
optional

2 vanilla beans, split in half,
seeds scraped

Method

- Cut the fresh figs and throw away any blemished or overripe fruits. Place the figs and vanilla bean seeds and pods in a 6–8 litre saucepan. I use a shallow baking dish.
- Slowly bring the figs to a rapid boil, then simmer for 20–30 minutes until figs are tender. Stir regularly and take care not to burn the figs. Water may be added if the fruit looks dry. Make sure the figs are soft before adding the sugar.
- Add all of the sugar and lemon juice.
- Bring all to a rapid boil for 15–20 minutes. The mixture must be quite thick and will start to turn a dark tan colour. You can remove the vanilla bean pods if you wish.
- Ladle the fig jam into sterilised jars, leave about a 1cm (½in) gap from the top and close the lid tightly.

 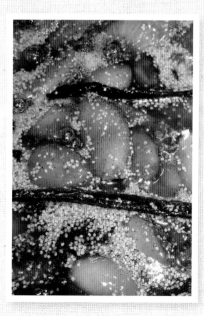

candied citrus skins infused with whole vanilla beans

My aunty taught me the original way of candying whole citrus fruit slices, which I have modified to produce my candied peels or skins, without the flesh. This method of candying citrus skins will give you the most 'jewel'-like and best-tasting citrus skins, with only a small hint of bitterness. It also keeps well for months in the fridge.

The use of salted water in this recipe is to soften and reduce the bitterness of the peels. It also helps the sugar syrup to penetrate the skins, allowing the 'candying' to occur faster.

Ingredients

1000g (35½oz) oranges or grapefruit

700g (25oz) raw sugar

2–3 vanilla beans, split in half, seeds scraped

2 teaspoons fine sea salt

700g (25oz) raw sugar

medium size lemon, juiced

Method

- The best way to prepare the fruit skins is to juice all the fruits first, then remove all the membranes, leaving the whole two halves of the orange or grapefruit. Cut these halves into quarters or eights
- Cover the citrus skins with water completely and scatter with the sea salt. Leave to soak for one hour or overnight.
- Throw away the salted water and rinse thoroughly with cold water.
- Cover the citrus skins with clean cool water, and cook on medium heat on a rolling boil for 10 minutes. Let it cool for a few hours.
- Throw away the water and rinse the peels thoroughly. Cover with clean, cool water and boil again until it comes to a rolling boil. Check if the peels are soft, but not mushy. They must still hold their shape.
- Throw away most of the water, leaving about 500ml (17fl oz) of water.
- Add the raw sugar, the vanilla beans (scrape out the seeds, but include all skins) and the lemon juice (this will prevent the syrup crystallising).
- Boil gently and stir frequently until the syrup is reduced and the pieces of citrus skin are translucent.
- Leave the candied citrus skins in the syrup and let cool completely before storing them in the fridge.
- Alternatively, quickly put candied skins and syrup into sterilised jars, leave about a 1cm (½in) gap from the top and close the lid tightly.

Top: cumquats and Cointreau marmalade
Middle: candied citrus skins infused with whole vanilla beans
Bottom: fig preserve infused with vanilla bean

fig, olive and walnut tapenade

Once you have made the fig preserve, you can make this fantastic tapenade.
Take care not to overprocess your tapenade, you do not want to end up with a paste.
Use the 'pulse' function rather than the 'on' button.

Ingredients

100g (3.5oz) fig preserve

100g (3$\frac{1}{2}$oz) kalamata olives in brine, pitted

75g (2$\frac{1}{2}$oz) walnuts

1 tablespoon walnut oil

Method

- Crush walnuts in a food processor for a few seconds, using a pulsing action, until they are roughly crushed. Do not over crush the walnuts to form a paste. Move crushed walnuts to a medium-sized bowl.
- Pulverise the olives and fig preserve together, using the pulsing action of a food processor.
- Tip the olive and fig rough paste onto the crushed walnuts, add the walnut oil and mix well.
- Serve with crisp sourdough crackers and shavings of parmesan cheese.

Note: You can substitute the fig preserve with 100g (3.5oz) of cumquat preserve

cucumber yoghurt dip

You have to start this recipe overnight to drain the yoghurt. I prefer to use dried mint for this dip to give a stronger but more mellow mint flavour. If you like fresh mint, substitute 1 heaped tablespoon of chopped fresh mint. Crushed dried chilli can be added for some 'fire' if you wish.

Ingredients

500g (18oz) Greek-style full cream yoghurt, preferably organic (the creamiest/thickest one you can find)

1 Lebanese cucumber (about 150–200g/7oz)

1–2 cloves of garlic, finely crushed (optional)

1 tablespoon extra virgin olive oil

1 teaspoon dried mint

1 teaspoon sea-salt flakes, the best you can find

Method

- About 12 hours prior to serving, drain the yoghurt in a moistened cheesecloth or a fine colander over a deep bowl. Place the bowl in the fridge to drain to avoid spoilage.
- Grate the cucumber (with or without the skin, as you like it) and using your fingers squeeze as much juice as possible. Leave to drain further in a fine colander, with a sprinkle of salt. Salt further draws the water out of the cucumber. Leave for half an hour.
- In a small bowl, place the drained yoghurt and cucumber, olive oil, crushed garlic, mint and salt and mix well.
- Taste and adjust according to your personal taste, then leave for an hour or two for the flavour to develop.
- Serve with sourdough lavash or sesame grizzini.

Variation: Add some cooked and drained spinach or 2 small stalks of celery, chopped into fine cubes.

chickpea and sesame dip (hummus)

Hummus has become the universal dip. It is available everywhere, including your local supermarket. However, nothing beats your very own hummus, made with love, using the best organic ingredients, free of canola oil and additives or preservatives of any kind. I love garlic but I am not keen on the pungent taste and flavour of raw garlic in this 'creamy soothing' flavour that is hummus, so I always roast my garlic lightly until it becomes soft and caramelised, rendering a sumptuous garlic flavour without the sharp pungency.

Ingredients

400g (14oz) cooked organic chickpeas

$\frac{1}{2}$ cup chickpea cooking liquid

2–3 clove of garlic, lightly roasted until soft

$\frac{1}{3}$ cup hulled sesame paste (tahini)

$\frac{1}{4}$ teaspoon ground cummin

$\frac{1}{4}$ teaspoon ground sweet paprika (optional)

1 teaspoon (5g) sea salt flakes, the best you can find

Juice of two medium lemons

Method

- About 12 hours prior to serving, or the night before, wash and soak the chickpeas in filtered water or whey with a squeeze of lemon.
- Replace the soaking water with 3 cups of fresh filtered water, bring the chickpeas to the boil, cover and lower the heat. Cook until chickpeas are soft.
- Check from time to time to make sure the water has not completely evaporated, add boiling water to top up, if necessary.
- Drain the chickpeas, leaving about half a cup of the cooking water. Place the chickpeas and water in a food processor and pulse until creamy. This will take a while.
- Do not add any other ingredients until the chickpeas are ready.
- When ready, add the rest of the ingredients, starting with the roasted garlic, tahini, lemon, cummin and salt in the food processor.
- Taste and adjust according to your personal taste, then leave for an hour or two for the flavours to come together. Drizzle with extra olive oil and a sprinkle of cumin and paprika, if you wish.
- Serve with sourdough lavash or sesame grizzini.

Note: The mixture will thicken as it cools.

Variation: Use cooked broad beans or butter beans to replace the chickpeas.

Acknowledgements

This book is dedicated, first and foremost, to my dearest Graeme and my beloved daughter, Dechen. You both have made it possible for me to write this book in peace and allowed me the time to bake, bake and bake some more.

Graeme, without your groundedness and constant enthusiasm, I would have never have had the courage to teach, which started my whole sourdough journey. You have taught me to live and work my passion. Thank you!

Dechen, you are my little angel, thank you for allowing those times away from playing with you. You have such an amazing ability to amuse yourself for hours, including talking to our dogs, kikki and grommit. You are the love of my life!

My deepest gratitude goes to Linda Williams for trusting me to write this book. Your love for my sourdough bread helped me create my dream of writing this book and you made it happen for me.

Thank you for my lifelines and soul-helpers: my parents, as well as Merva, Trish, Terri, Jenny, Emmy, Ocean, Donna. Your endless support and belief in me at those times when I doubted myself is deeply appreciated and felt.

My profound gratitude and deep affection for Merva and Dhillon for rescuing me in more ways than one.

A heartfelt tribute to Jude Blereau and Jane McCaffrey for giving me the 'kick', support and belief I needed to start this journey into teaching what I love.

Thank you to my amazing editor, Diane Jardine, you are my angel! Millions of thanks for putting your very best into this book and for guiding me through the whole process.

Thanks a million Hayley Norman for such magnificent and creative work in designing this book, you are such a delight to work with.

To Graeme Gillies, thank you so much for capturing in pictures the essence of each of my sourdough breads and for caputuring my joyous spirit in my photograph.

A very special thank you for my beloved Shaun O'Sullivan for loving me and making it possible for me to complete the last leg of this book's journey.

Thank you for the love and support from all my students who have taught me the most and made me explore new frontiers in sourdough breadmaking I never thought possible.

Greatest gratitude for those of you (you know who you are), too many to mention, for being around me, supporting and loving me whenever I need you.

Last but not least, thank you for the love of the Divine, who is always present in me and those around me, and therefore makes it possible for me to do what I am supposed to do in this life.

About the author

Following successful careers in fashion and finance, Yoke Mardewi took the plunge and decided to work at her first love and passion—the making and sharing of food, in particular, sourdough bread-making.

Yoke runs cooking classes with a specialty in sourdough breadmaking. She has featured on Western Australian TV, radio and in various food and health websites, newspapers and magazines. Her cooking classes are as much about sharing her warmth and passion for life as they are about the joy of food.

She is a member of the Artisan Bakers Association and Slow Food. She is a keen supporter of organic/biodynamic farming.

She currently lives in Perth with her daughter and two jack russells. She supports and encourages others to have the courage to pursue their passion in life.

www.wildsourdough.com.au
Yoke can be contacted at:
yoke.wildsourdough@gmail.com
or wildsourdough@highway1.com.au

Index (for recipes, see Contents page)

First published in Australia in 2009 by
New Holland Publishers (Australia) Pty Ltd
Sydney • Auckland • London • Cape Town

1/66 Gibbes Street, Chatswood NSW 2067 Australia
www.newholland.com.au
218 Lake Road Northcote Auckland 0746 New Zealand
86 Edgware Road London W2 2EA United Kingdom
80 McKenzie Street Cape Town 8001 South Africa

Copyright © 2009 in text: Yoke Mardewi
Copyright © 2009 New Holland Publishers (Australia) Pty Ltd
Pages 25–28 Copyright © Celiac Sprue Association

All rights reserved. No part of this publication may be reproduced, stored in a retrieval system
or transmitted, in any form or by any means, electronic, mechanical, photocopying, recording
or otherwise, without the prior written permission of the publishers and copyright holders.

A record of this book is available from the National Library of Australia.

ISBN 9781741107449

Publisher: Fiona Schultz and Linda Williams
Publishing Manager: Lliane Clarke
Project Editor: Diane Jardine
Designer: Hayley Norman
Food photography: Graeme Gillies
Incidental photography: Yoke Mardewi
Printer: SNP Leefung Printing Co. Ltd (China)

10 9 8 7 6 5 4 3 2 1